Teach Yourself
VISUALLY™
Photoshop® 6

by Mike Wooldridge

Visual™

D1385124

From
maranGraphics™

&

Hungry Minds™

HUNGRY MINDS, INC.
New York, NY ♦ Cleveland, OH ♦ Indianapolis, IN

Teach Yourself VISUALLY™ Photoshop® 6

Published by
Hungry Minds, Inc.
909 Third Avenue
New York, NY 10022
Original Text and Original Illustrations Copyright © 2001 Hungry Minds, Inc.
Design and certain of the illustrations Copyright © 1992-2001 maranGraphics, Inc.
5755 Coopers Avenue
Mississauga, Ontario, Canada
L4Z 1R9

Library of Congress Control Number: 00-107557
ISBN: 0-7645-3513-7

Printed in the United States of America
10 9 8 7 6 5 4 3 2
1K/SY/QZ/QR/IN
Distributed in the United States by Hungry Minds, Inc.

Distributed by CDG Books Canada Inc. for Canada; by Transworld Publishers Limited in the United Kingdom; by IDG Norge Books for Norway; by IDG Sweden Books for Sweden; by IDG Books Australia Publishing Corporation Pty. Ltd. for Australia and New Zealand; by TransQuest Publishers Pte Ltd. for Singapore, Malaysia, Thailand, Indonesia, and Hong Kong; by Gotop Information Inc. for Taiwan; by ICG Muse, Inc. for Japan; by Intersoft for South Africa; by Eyrolles for France; by International Thomson Publishing for Germany, Austria and Switzerland; by Distribuidora Cuspide for Argentina; by LR International for Brazil; by Galileo Libros for Chile; by Ediciones ZETA S.C.R. Ltda. for Peru; by WS Computer Publishing Corporation, Inc., for the Philippines; by Contemporanea de Ediciones for Venezuela; by Express Computer Distributors for the Caribbean and West Indies; by Micronesia Media Distributor, Inc. for Micronesia; by Chips Computadoras S.A. de C.V. for Mexico; by Editorial Norma de Panama S.A. for Panama; by American Bookshops for Finland.

For corporate orders, please call maranGraphics at 800-469-6616 or fax 905-890-9434.
For general information on Hungry Minds' products and services please contact our Customer Care Department within the U.S. at 800-762-2974, outside the U.S. at 317-572-3993 or fax 317-572-4002.
For sales inquiries and reseller information, including discounts, premium and bulk quantity sales, and foreign-language translations, please contact our Customer Care Department at 800-434-3422, fax 317-572-4002, or write to Hungry Minds, Inc., Attn: Customer Care Department, 10475 Crosspoint Boulevard, Indianapolis, IN 46256.
For information on licensing foreign or domestic rights, please contact our Sub-Rights Customer Care Department at 212-884-5000.
For information on using Hungry Minds' products and services in the classroom or for ordering examination copies, please contact our Educational Sales Department at 800-434-2086 or fax 317-572-4005.
Please contact our Public Relations Department at 212-884-5163 for press review copies or 212-884-5000 for author interviews and other publicity information or fax 212-884-5400.
For authorization to photocopy items for corporate, personal, or educational use, please contact Copyright Clearance Center, 222 Rosewood Drive, Danvers, MA 01923, or fax 978-750-4470.

Screen shots displayed in this book are based on prereleased software and are subject to change.

Trademark Acknowledgments

Permissions

Hungry Minds™ is a trademark of Hungry Minds, Inc.

U.S. Corporate Sales	**U.S. Trade Sales**
Contact maranGraphics at (800) 469-6616 or Fax (905) 890-9434.	Contact Hungry Minds at (800) 434-3422 or Fax (317) 572-4002.

ABOUT IDG BOOKS WORLDWIDE

Welcome to the world of IDG Books Worldwide.

IDG Books Worldwide, Inc., is a subsidiary of International Data Group, the world's largest publisher of computer-related information and the leading global provider of information services on information technology. IDG was founded more than 30 years ago by Patrick J. McGovern and now employs more than 9,000 people worldwide. IDG publishes more than 290 computer publications in over 75 countries. More than 90 million people read one or more IDG publications each month.

Launched in 1990, IDG Books Worldwide is today the #1 publisher of best-selling computer books in the United States. We are proud to have received eight awards from the Computer Press Association in recognition of editorial excellence and three from Computer Currents' First Annual Readers' Choice Awards. Our best-selling ...For Dummies® series has more than 50 million copies in print with translations in 31 languages. IDG Books Worldwide, through a joint venture with IDG's Hi-Tech Beijing, became the first U.S. publisher to publish a computer book in the People's Republic of China. In record time, IDG Books Worldwide has become the first choice for millions of readers around the world who want to learn how to better manage their businesses.

Our mission is simple: Every one of our books is designed to bring extra value and skill-building instructions to the reader. Our books are written by experts who understand and care about our readers. The knowledge base of our editorial staff comes from years of experience in publishing, education, and journalism — experience we use to produce books to carry us into the new millennium. In short, we care about books, so we attract the best people. We devote special attention to details such as audience, interior design, use of icons, and illustrations. And because we use an efficient process of authoring, editing, and desktop publishing our books electronically, we can spend more time ensuring superior content and less time on the technicalities of making books.

You can count on our commitment to deliver high-quality books at competitive prices on topics you want to read about. At IDG Books Worldwide, we continue in the IDG tradition of delivering quality for more than 30 years. You'll find no better book on a subject than one from IDG Books Worldwide.

John J. Kilcullen
John Kilcullen
Chairman and CEO
IDG Books Worldwide, Inc.

Eighth Annual Computer Press Awards ≥ 1992

Ninth Annual Computer Press Awards ≥ 1993

Tenth Annual Computer Press Awards ≥ 1994

Eleventh Annual Computer Press Awards ≥ 1995

IDG is the world's leading IT media, research and exposition company. Founded in 1964, IDG had 1997 revenues of $2.05 billion and has more than 9,000 employees worldwide. IDG offers the widest range of media options that reach IT buyers in 75 countries representing 95% of worldwide IT spending. IDG's diverse product and services portfolio spans six key areas including print publishing, online publishing, expositions and conferences, market research, education and training, and global marketing services. More than 90 million people read one or more of IDG's 290 magazines and newspapers, including IDG's leading global brands — Computerworld, PC World, Network World, Macworld and the Channel World family of publications. IDG Books Worldwide is one of the fastest-growing computer book publishers in the world, with more than 700 titles in 36 languages. The "...For Dummies®" series alone has more than 50 million copies in print. IDG offers online users the largest network of technology-specific Web sites around the world through IDG.net (http://www.idg.net), which comprises more than 225 targeted Web sites in 55 countries worldwide. International Data Corporation (IDC) is the world's largest provider of information technology data, analysis and consulting, with research centers in over 41 countries and more than 400 research analysts worldwide. IDG World Expo is a leading producer of more than 168 globally branded conferences and expositions in 35 countries including E3 (Electronic Entertainment Expo), Macworld Expo, ComNet, Windows World Expo, ICE (Internet Commerce Expo), Agenda, DEMO, and Spotlight. IDG's training subsidiary, ExecuTrain, is the world's largest computer training company, with more than 230 locations worldwide and 785 training courses. IDG Marketing Services helps industry-leading IT companies build international brand recognition by developing global integrated marketing programs via IDG's print, online and exposition products worldwide. Further information about the company can be found at www.idg.com.
1/26/00

maranGraphics is a family-run business
located near Toronto, Canada.

At **maranGraphics**, we believe in producing great computer books — one book at a time.

maranGraphics has been producing high-technology products for over 25 years, which enables us to offer the computer book community a unique communication process.

Our computer books use an integrated communication process, which is very different from the approach used in other computer books. Each spread is, in essence, a flow chart — the text and screen shots are totally incorporated into the layout of the spread. Introductory text and helpful tips complete the learning experience.

maranGraphics' approach encourages the left and right sides of the brain to work together —resulting in faster orientation and greater memory retention.

Above all, we are very proud of the handcrafted nature of our books. Our carefully-chosen writers are experts in their fields, and spend countless hours researching and organizing the content for each topic. Our artists rebuild every screen shot to provide the best clarity possible, making our screen shots the most precise and easiest to read in the

industry. We strive for perfection, and believe that the time spent handcrafting each element results in the best computer books money can buy.

Thank you for purchasing this book. We hope you enjoy it!

Sincerely,

Robert Maran
President
maranGraphics
Rob@maran.com
www.maran.com
www.idgbooks.com/visual

CREDITS

Acquisitions, Editorial, and Media Development

Project Editor
Dana Rhodes Lesh

Acquisitions Editor
Martine Edwards

Product Development Supervisor
Lindsay Sandman

Copy Editor
Tim Borek

Technical Editor
Lee Musick

Editorial Manager
Rev Mengle

Media Development Manager
Laura Carpenter

Editorial Assistants:
Candace Nicholson, Amanda Foxworth

Production

Book Design
maranGraphics™

Project Coordinator
Maridee Ennis

Layout
Joe Bucki, Sean Decker, LeAndra Johnson,
Barry Offringa, Kristin Pickett, Erin Zeltner

Screen Artists
Craig Dearing, Mark Harris, Jill A. Johnson

Illustrators
Ronda David-Burroughs, David E. Gregory,
maranGraphics™

Proofreaders
Susan Moritz, Christine Pingleton, Charles Spencer

Indexer
York Production Services, Inc.

Special Help
Ted Cains, Jill Mazurczyk

ACKNOWLEDGMENTS

General and Administrative

IDG Books Worldwide, Inc.: John Kilcullen, CEO; Bill Barry, President and COO; John Ball, Executive VP, Operations & Administration; John Harris, CFO

IDG Books Technology Publishing Group: Richard Swadley, Senior Vice President and Publisher; Mary Bednarek, Vice President and Publisher; Walter R. Bruce III, Vice President and Publisher; Joseph Wikert, Vice President and Publisher; Mary C. Corder, Editorial Director; Andy Cummings, Publishing Director, General User Group; Barry Pruett, Publishing Director

IDG Books Manufacturing: Ivor Parker, Vice President, Manufacturing

IDG Books Marketing: John Helmus, Assistant Vice President, Director of Marketing

IDG Books Online Management: Brenda McLaughlin, Executive Vice President, Chief Internet Officer; Gary Millrood, Executive Vice President of Business Development, Sales and Marketing

IDG Books Packaging: Marc J. Mikulich, Vice President, Brand Strategy and Research

IDG Books Production for Branded Press: Debbie Stailey, Production Director

IDG Books Sales: Roland Elgey, Senior Vice President, Sales and Marketing; Michael Violano, Vice President,

The publisher would like to give special thanks to Patrick J. McGovern,
without whom this book would not have been possible

ABOUT THE AUTHOR

Mike Wooldridge is a technology writer, Web designer, and educator in Berkeley, California. He is also the author of *Teach Yourself Visually Dreamweaver 3*.

AUTHOR'S ACKNOWLEDGMENTS

Thanks to Martine Edwards for the opportunity to write my second book; Project Editor Dana Lesh for her patience and guidance; Copy Editor Tim Borek for his careful work; and Lee Musick for his technical editing. Also, thanks to Craig Dearing, Jill Johnson, Mark Harris, David Gregory, Ronda David-Burroughs, and Maridee Ennis.

To Griffin, my one-year-old son who really likes to play
with the mouse and keyboard.

TABLE OF CONTENTS

Chapter 1

Chapter 2

Chapter 3

Chapter 4

MAKING SELECTIONS

Chapter 5

MANIPULATING SELECTIONS

TABLE OF CONTENTS

Chapter 6

SPECIFYING COLOR MODES

Chapter 7

PAINTING WITH COLOR

Chapter 8

ADJUSTING COLORS

Chapter 9

WORKING WITH LAYERS

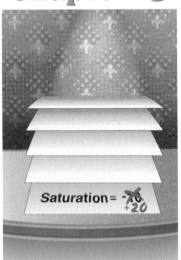

Chapter 10

APPLYING LAYER EFFECTS

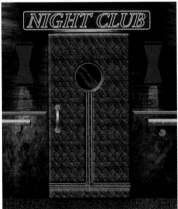

TABLE OF CONTENTS

Chapter 11

APPLYING FILTERS

Chapter 12

ADDING AND MANIPULATING TYPE

Chapter 13

AUTOMATING YOUR WORK

Chapter 14

SAVING FILES

Chapter 15

PRINTING IMAGES

Chapter 16

PERFORMANCE TIPS

CHAPTER 1

Getting Started

Are you interested in creating, modifying, combining, and optimizing digital photos and other images on your computer? This chapter introduces you to Adobe Photoshop, a popular software application for working with digital images.

WORK WITH IMAGES

Photoshop lets you create, modify, combine, and optimize digital images.

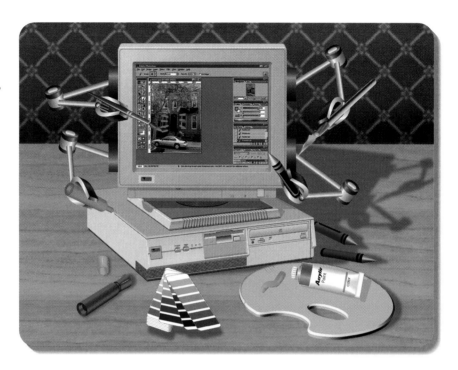

MANIPULATE PHOTOS

As its name suggests, Photoshop excels at editing digital photographs. You can use the program to make subtle changes, such as to adjust the color in a scanned photo, or you can use its elaborate filters to make your snapshots look like abstract art.

PAINT PICTURES

Photoshop's painting features make it a formidable illustration tool as well as a photo editor. You can apply colors or patterns to your images with a variety of brush styles. In addition, you can use Photoshop's typographic tools to integrate stylized letters and words into your images.

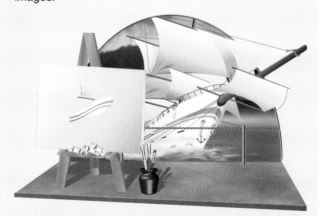

CREATE A DIGITAL COLLAGE

You can combine different image elements in Photoshop. Your compositions can include photos, scanned art, text, and anything else you can save on your computer as a digital image. By putting elements in Photoshop onto separate layers, you can move, transform, and customize them independently of one another.

ORGANIZE YOUR PHOTOS

Photoshop offers useful ways to keep your images organized after you have edited them. You can archive your images on contact sheets or display them in a Web photo gallery.

PUT YOUR IMAGES TO WORK

After you edit your work, you can use your images in a variety of ways. Photoshop lets you print your images, save them in a format suitable for use on a Web page, or prepare them for use in a page-layout program.

UNDERSTAND PHOTOSHOP

Photoshop's tools let you move, color, stylize, and add text to elements of your images.

UNDERSTAND PIXELS

Digital images in Photoshop are made up of tiny, solid-color squares called *pixels*. Photoshop works its magic by rearranging and recoloring these squares. If you zoom in close, you can see the pixels that make up your image. (Use the Zoom tool, described in Chapter 2.)

CHOOSE YOUR PIXELS

To edit specific pixels in your image, you first have to select them by using one of Photoshop's selection tools (see Chapter 4). Photoshop also has a number of commands that help you select specific parts of your image, including commands that expand or contract your existing selection or select pixels of a specific color.

PAINT

After you have selected your pixels, you can apply color to them by using Photoshop's Paintbrush, Airbrush, and Pencil tools. You can also fill your selections with solid or semitransparent colors. Painting is covered in Chapter 7.

ADJUST COLOR

You can brighten, darken, and change the hue of colors in parts of your image with Photoshop's Dodge, Burn, and similar tools. Other commands display interactive dialog boxes that let you make wholesale color adjustments, letting you precisely correct overly dark or light digital photographs. See Chapter 8 for details.

APPLY EFFECTS AND FILTERS

Photoshop's effects let you easily add drop shadows, 3D shading, and other styles to your images. You can also perform complex color manipulations or distortions by using Photoshop filters. Filters can make your image look like an impressionist painting, apply sharpening or blurring, or distort your image in various ways. Chapters 10 and 11 cover effects and filters.

ADD TYPE

Photoshop's type tools enable you to easily apply titles and labels to your images. You can combine these tools with Photoshop's special effects commands to create warped, 3D, or wildly colored type. You can find out more about type in Chapter 12.

GET IMAGES

You can get raw material
for using Photoshop from
a variety of sources.

START FROM SCRATCH

You can create your Photoshop image from scratch by
opening a blank canvas in the image window. (See
"Create a New Image" in this chapter.) Then you can
apply color and patterns with Photoshop's painting tools
or cut and paste parts of other images to create a
composite.

SCANNED PHOTOS AND ART

A scanner gives you an inexpensive way to convert
existing paper-based content into digital form. You can
scan photos and art into your computer, retouch and
stylize them in Photoshop, and then output them to a
color printer.

CLIP ART

If you want a wide variety of image content to work with,
consider buying a clip art collection. Such collections
usually include illustrations, photos, and decorative icons
that you can use in imaging projects. Most software
stores sell clip art; you can also buy downloadable clip
art online.

DIGITAL PHOTOS

Digital cameras are a great way to get digital images onto
your computer. Most digital cameras save their images in
JPEG or TIFF format, both of which can be opened and
edited in Photoshop. The program's color adjustment
tools are great for correcting color and exposure flaws in
digital camera images.

You can use a combination of tools, menu commands, and palette-based features to create and edit your images in Photoshop.

USING PHOTOSHOP'S WORKSPACE

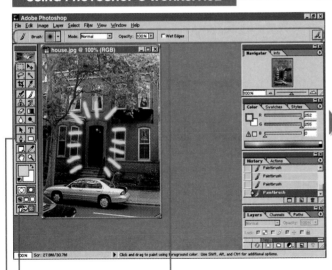

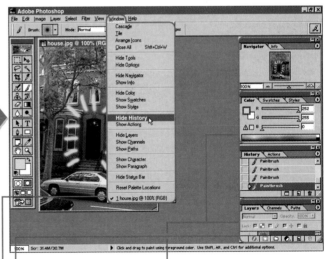

■ Each image you open in Photoshop is displayed in its own window.

■ Photoshop's toolbox displays a variety of icons, each one representing an image-editing tool. You click

and drag inside your image to apply most of the tools.

■ The Options bar displays controls that let you customize the selected tool in the toolbox.

■ Some Photoshop features are organized in small, free-floating windows called *palettes*.

■ You can show and hide the palettes with the Windows menu.

■ The Color palette lets you select the painting color.

■ The Layers palette lets you arrange and manipulate the different layers in a multilayered image. (See Chapter 9.)

SET PREFERENCES

Photoshop's Preferences dialog boxes let you change default settings and customize how the program looks.

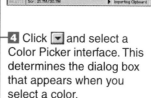

SET PREFERENCES

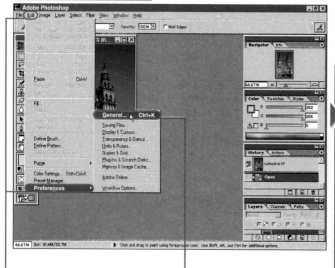

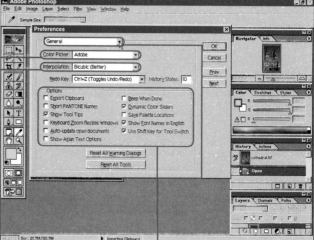

1 Click **Edit**.

2 Click **Preferences**.

3 Click **General**.

4 Click ▾ and select a Color Picker interface. This determines the dialog box that appears when you select a color.

5 Click ▾ and select an interpolation type.

6 Click the interface options you want to use (☐ changes to ☑).

7 Click ▾ and select **Display & Cursors**.

**What type of measurement units
should I use in Photoshop?**

Typically, you should use the units
most applicable to the type of
output you are interested in. Pixel
units are useful for Web imaging
because screen dimensions are
measured in pixels. Inches or
picas are useful for print because
those are standards for working
on paper.

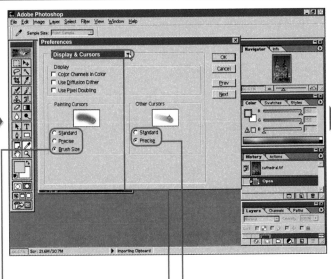

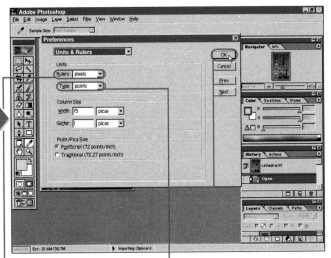

■ The Display & Cursors
Preferences options appear.

8 Click a cursor type to use
for the painting tools (the
paintbrush, eraser, and
others) (○ changes to ◉).

9 Click a cursor type to
use for the other tools
(○ changes to ◉).

10 Click ▼ and select **Units
& Rulers**.

■ The Units & Rulers
Preferences options appear.

11 Click ▼ and select the
units to be displayed on the
window rulers. These units
will also be the default units
selected when you resize an
image.

12 Click ▼ and select the
default units for type.

13 Click **OK** to close the
Preferences dialog box.

CALIBRATE YOUR MONITOR

You can calibrate your monitor to ensure that colors display accurately and reliably when you use Photoshop.

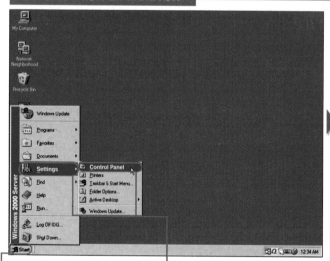

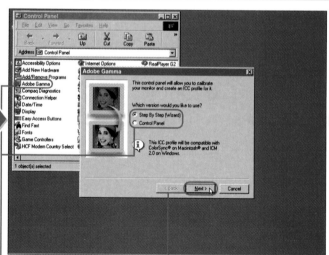

Note: For best results, let your monitor warm up for at least a half hour before calibrating. Also, make sure that your monitor is set to display thousands of colors or more.

1 Click **Start**.

2 Click **Settings**.

3 Click **Control Panel**.

■ On a Macintosh, choose **Control Panels** from the Apple menu.

4 Double-click the Adobe Gamma icon.

5 Click an option to select an interface (○ changes to ◉).

Note: The Step By Step option provides a wizard to help calibrate your monitor. The Control Panel option lets you perform all the calibrations in a single dialog box (and is recommended only if you are a calibration expert).

6 Click **Next**.

How should I calibrate my monitor if I am working collaboratively?

If you are working on a Photoshop project with others — for instance, with other artists or with a printing company — it is a good idea for everyone to calibrate his or her monitor to a single standard. For instance, have everyone select the same 5000-Kelvin setting for the monitor's white point value.

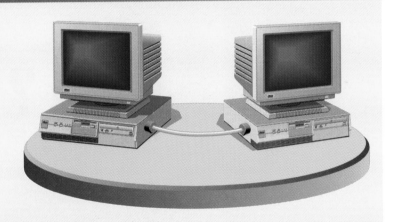

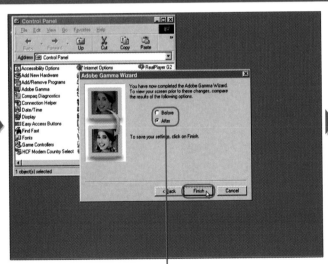

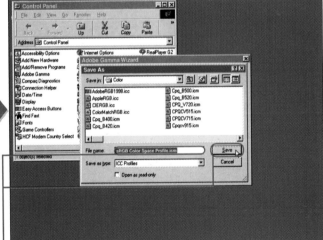

■ If you selected Step By Step, Photoshop walks you through several monitor calibration steps.

■ At the end of the Step By Step, you can toggle between your original and new calibration settings.

7 Click **Finish**.

8 Type a name for your profile.

9 Click **Save**.

Note: If you have strict color requirements for your work, you should recalibrate your monitor every few months.

GET HELP

Photoshop comes with extensive documentation that you can access on your computer in case you ever need help.

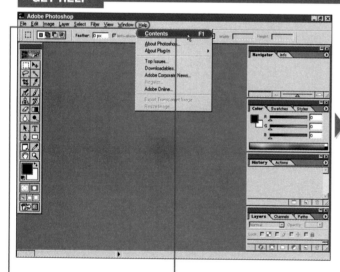

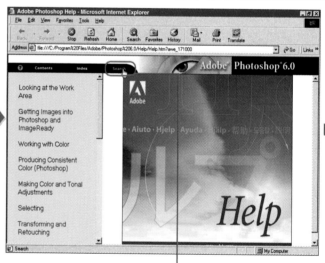

1 Click **Help**.

2 Click **Contents**.

■ Photoshop opens a Web browser and displays the Help interface.

3 Click **Search** to search for information about a particular topic.

How can I get additional tips and news about Photoshop?

Click **Help** and then **Adobe Online** to access information about product support, software upgrades, and third-party add-ons for Photoshop. You need an Internet connection to get information via Adobe Online. Click **Refresh** to make sure that you have the latest software to use this feature.

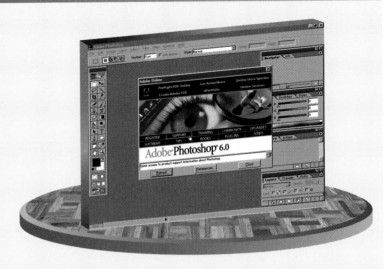

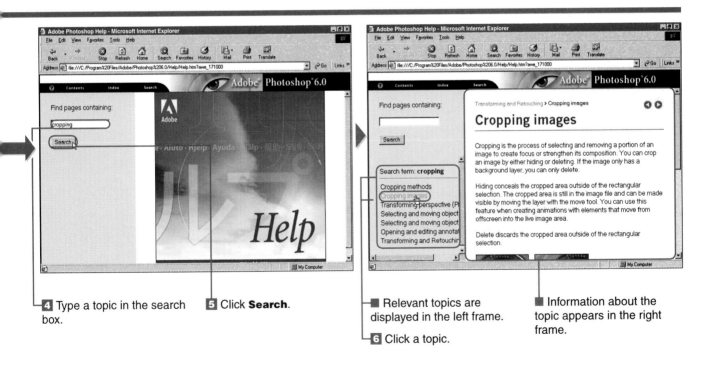

■4 Type a topic in the search box.

■5 Click **Search**.

■ Relevant topics are displayed in the left frame.

■6 Click a topic.

■ Information about the topic appears in the right frame.

OPEN AN IMAGE

You can open an existing image file in Photoshop.

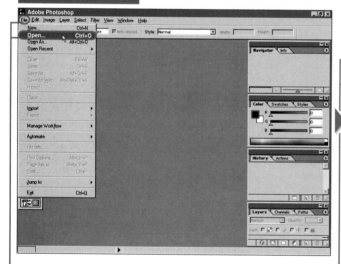

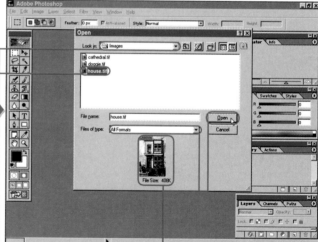

1 Click **File**.

2 Click **Open**.

■ The Open dialog box appears.

3 Click ▼ and browse to the folder that contains the image you want to open.

4 Click the filename of the image you want to open.

■ A preview of the image is displayed.

■ To limit the types of files listed, click ▼ and select a format from the Files of Type drop-down list.

5 Click **Open**.

What types of files can Photoshop open?

Photoshop can open most of the image file
formats in common use today. Here are a few
of the more popular ones:

BMP (Bitmap)	The standard Windows image format
PICT	The standard Macintosh image format
TIFF (Tagged Image File Format)	A popular format for print on Windows and Macintosh
EPS (Encapsulated PostScript)	Another print-oriented format
JPEG (Joint Photographic Experts Group)	A format for Web images
GIF (Graphics Interchage Format)	Another format for Web images
PSD (Photoshop Document)	Photoshop's native file format

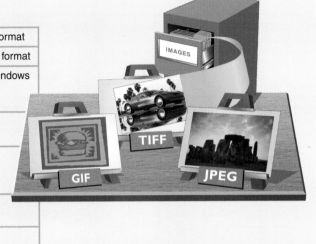

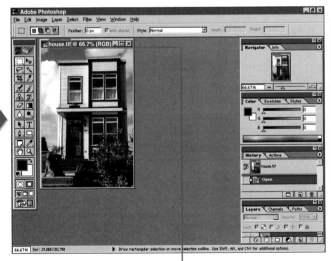

■ Photoshop opens the
image in a new window.

■ The filename appears in
the title bar.

**OPEN RECENTLY
ACCESSED IMAGES**

1 Click **File**.

2 Click **Open Recent** to
view a list of files that you
recently worked on.

3 Click the filename of the
image that you want to open.

■ Photoshop opens the
image in a new window.

CREATE A NEW IMAGE

You can start a
Photoshop project by
creating a blank image.

CREATE A NEW IMAGE

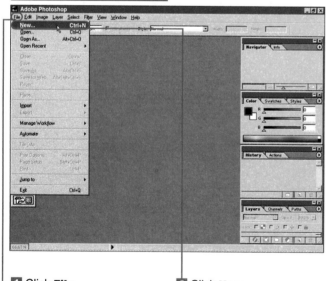

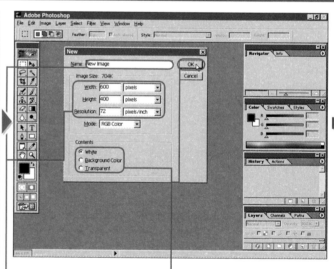

1 Click **File**.

2 Click **New**.

3 Type a name for the new image.

4 Type in the desired dimensions and resolution.

5 Click the type of pixels the new image will be initially made up of (○ changes to ●).

6 Click **OK**.

How do I choose a resolution for a new image?

The appropriate resolution depends on how the image will eventually be used. For Web or multimedia images, select 72 pixels/inch (the standard resolution for on-screen images). For black-and-white images to be printed on regular paper on a laser printer, 150 pixels/inch probably suffices. For full-color magazine or brochure images, you should use a higher resolution — at least 250 pixels/inch.

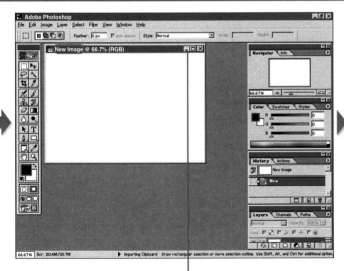

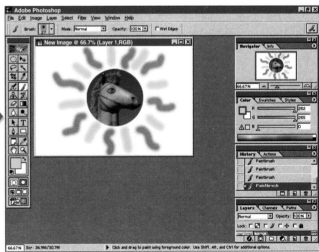

■ Photoshop creates a new image window at the specified dimensions.

■ The filename appears in the title bar.

7 Use Photoshop's tools and commands to create your image.

■ In this example, part of another image has been cut and pasted into the window, and color streaks were added with the paintbrush tool.

Note: To find out how to save your image, see Chapter 14.

CHAPTER 2

Understanding Photoshop Basics

Are you ready to start working with images? This chapter shows you how to execute commands, select tools, and fine-tune your work space.

EXECUTE PHOTOSHOP COMMANDS

You can make changes to an image by executing a Photoshop command.

EXECUTE PHOTOSHOP COMMANDS

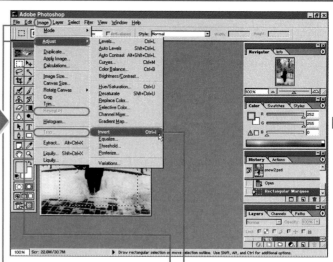

■1 Click a selection tool (for example, [::]).

■2 Click and drag to select the area of the image that you want to change.

■ Photoshop outlines the area with dashes.

Note: For more information about making selections, see Chapter 4.

■3 Click the menu that contains the command you want to perform (such as **Image**).

■4 If the command has a submenu, click it (such as **Adjust**).

■5 Click the command you want (such as **Invert**).

■ Photoshop grays out commands that do not apply to a current selection.

How do I stop a command in progress?

Press `Esc` (`⌘` + `.`) to halt a command. Stopping a command can be useful for commands that take a long time to execute, such as some filters (see Chapter 11).

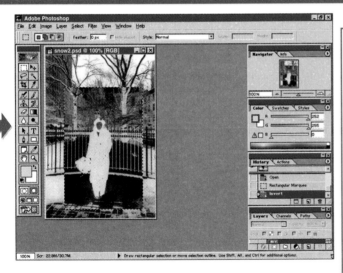

■ Photoshop applies the command to the selected area in the image.

Note: If you do not make a selection before executing a command, Photoshop applies the command to the entire image (or selected layer, depending on the command).

UNDO A COMMAND

■1 Click **Edit**.

■2 Click **Undo**.

■ The selection returns to its original state.

Note: You can use the History palette to undo multiple commands (see "Undo Commands or Revert to the Last Saved State").

Note: You can also press `Ctrl` + `Z` (`⌘` + `Z`) to undo a command.

MAGNIFY WITH THE ZOOM TOOL

You can change the
magnification of an
image with the Zoom
tool.

MAGNIFY WITH THE ZOOM TOOL

INCREASE MAGNIFICATION

■1 Click 🔍 (the Zoom tool).

■2 Click the image.

■ Photoshop increases the
magnification of the image.

Note: You can also press Ctrl *+* +
(⌘*+* +*) to increase magnification.*

■ The point that was clicked
in the image moves to the
center of the window.

■ The current magnification
is shown in the title bar and
status bar.

■ You can choose an exact
magnification by entering a
percentage value in the
status bar.

How do I quickly return an image to 100% magnification?

Double-click 🔍 in the toolbox, click **View** and then **Actual Pixels** from the menu, or press `Ctrl` + `Alt` + `0` (`⌘` + `option` + `0`).

DECREASE MAGNIFICATION

1 With 🔍 selected, press and hold `Alt` (`Option`) and click the image.

■ The original image was clicked to reduce the magnification to 66.7%.

Note: You can also press `Ctrl` + `−` (`⌘` + `−`) to decrease magnification.

MAGNIFY A DETAIL

1 Click and drag with 🔍 to select the detail.

■ The object appears enlarged on-screen.

ADJUST VIEWS WITH THE HAND TOOL

You can move an image within the window by using the Hand tool.

ADJUST VIEWS WITH THE HAND TOOL

1 Click 🖐 (the Hand tool).

Note: For the Hand tool to produce an effect, the image must be larger than the image window.

2 Click and drag inside the image window.

How can I quickly adjust the image window to see the entire image at its largest possible magnification on-screen?

Double-click , click **Fit On Screen** on the Options bar, or click **View** and then **Fit** from the menu to magnify the image to its largest possible size.

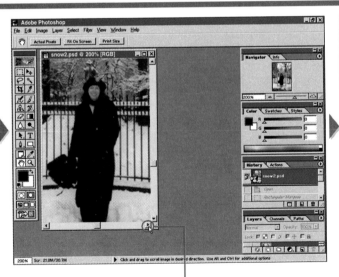

■ The view of the image shifts inside the window.

Note: The Hand tool is a more flexible alternative to using the scroll bars.

3 Click and hold the window's scroll bar button.

■ The image scrolls horizontally.

Note: Unlike the scroll bars, the Hand tool enables you to move the image freely in two dimensions.

CHANGE SCREEN MODES

You can switch the screen mode to change the look of your work space on-screen.

CHANGE SCREEN MODES

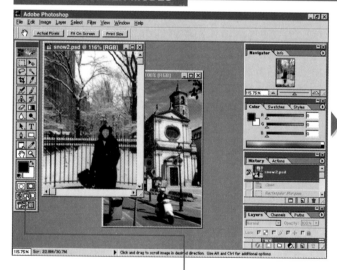

SWITCH TO FULL SCREEN WITH MENU

Note: The standard screen mode lets you view multiple images at once, each in a different window.

1 Click ▣ (the Full Screen Mode with Menu Bar button).

■ Photoshop puts the current image window in the center of a blank, full-screen canvas with the menu options at the top of the screen.

How do I display the menu bar when in Full Screen mode?

Press Shift + F to toggle the view of the menu bar in Full Screen mode.

SWITCH TO FULL SCREEN

1 Click ◻ (the Full Screen Mode button).

■ The image appears full screen without the menu.

CLOSE TOOLBOX AND PALETTES

1 Press Tab.

■ Photoshop closes all toolboxes and palettes.

Note: The Tab feature works in all of Photoshop's screen modes.

Note: To view the toolbox and palettes, you can press Tab again.

VIEW RULERS AND GUIDES

You can turn on rulers
and create guides, which
help you accurately place
elements in your image.

VIEW RULERS AND GUIDES

1 Click **View**.

2 Click **Show Rulers**.

■ Photoshop adds rulers to
the top and left sides of the
image window.

3 Click one of the rulers
and drag the cursor into
the window.

How do I change the units of my rulers?

Click **Edit**, **Preferences**, and then **Units & Rulers**. A dialog box appears that lets you change the units to pixels, inches, centimeters, points, picas, or percent.

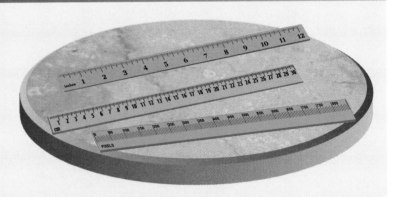

■ A thin colored line called a *guide* appears.

Note: Guides help you position the different elements that make up your Photoshop image. These lines do not appear on the printed image.

4 Click  (the Move tool) to adjust the placement of a guide.

5 Place the cursor over a guide and click and drag.

*Note: To align elements moved into an image with the guides, click **View** and then **Snap To Guides** from the drop-down menu.*

VIEW A GRID

You can turn on a grid that overlays your image. The grid is similar to a set of guides (see the section "View Rulers and Guides" in this chapter) and helps you organize elements within your image.

1 Click **View**.

2 Click **Show**.

3 Click **Grid**.

■ A grid appears on top of the image.

■ To adjust the space separating the grid lines, click **Edit**, **Preferences**, and then **Guides & Grid**.

*Note: When you click **View**, **Snap To**, and then **Grid**, elements in an image become aligned with the grid lines when they are moved close to them.*

USING SHORTCUTS TO SELECT TOOLS

You can press letter keys to select items in the toolbox. This can sometimes be more efficient than clicking on the tools.

USING SHORTCUTS TO SELECT TOOLS

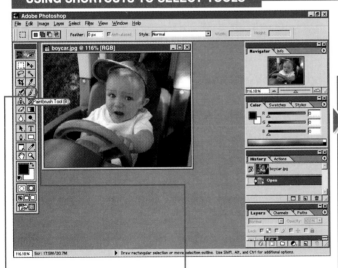

1 Place the cursor over a tool in the toolbox and hold it there (for example,).

■ A small box appears that describes the tool and gives its shortcut key.

Note: Each tool in the toolbox has a letter associated with it.

2 Press the indicated letter to select the tool (such as **B**).

■ The tool icon in the toolbox is selected and the cursor switches to the new tool.

Note: You can modify the shape of the cursor by adjusting Photoshop's Preferences settings (see Chapter 1).

Note: Following are shortcut keys for some common Photoshop tools:

Marquee	**M**	Move	**V**
Lasso	**L**	Paintbrush	**B**
Type	**T**	Zoom	**Z**

UNDO COMMANDS OR REVERT TO THE LAST SAVED STATE

You can undo multiple commands or revert to a previously saved state by using the history palette.

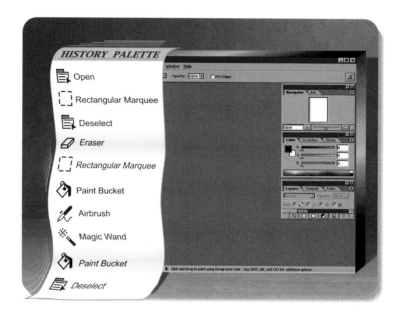

UNDO COMMANDS

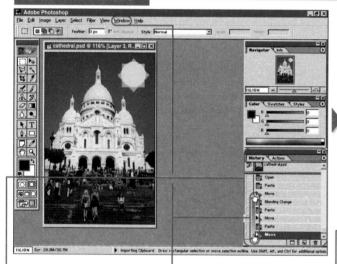

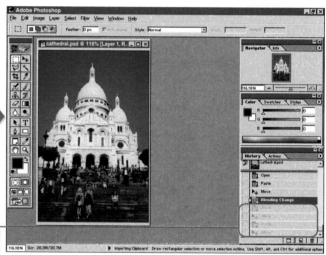

■ The History palette lists recently executed commands with the most recent command at the bottom.

■ If the History palette is not visible, you can click **Window** and then **Show History** to display it.

1 Click and drag the History slider upward (or click a previous command in the History palette).

■ Photoshop undoes the previous commands.

How does the History palette affect my computer's memory use?

Photoshop has to store image information for each command it remembers in the History palette. The accumulation of such saved commands can sometimes cause Photoshop to run out of memory. You can limit the number of commands Photoshop saves in the History palette in the Preferences settings (see Chapter 1). You can also free up memory by clicking **Edit**, **Purge**, and then **Histories**, which deletes the contents of the History palette.

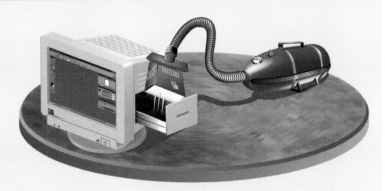

REVERT TO THE LAST SAVED STATE

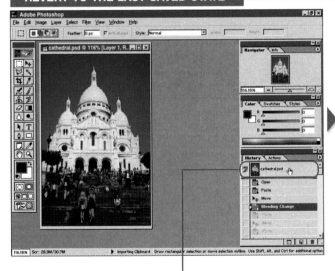

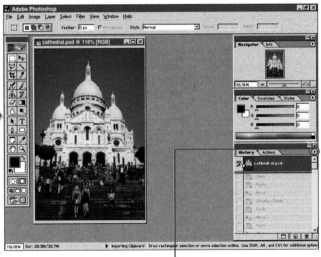

Note: Photoshop stores the last saved state as a snapshot at the top of the History palette.

■1 Click the snapshot image.

■ The image reverts to the last saved state.

■ You can add additional snapshots to the History palette as you work by clicking the History menu and then **New Snapshot**. You can then return to the previous image state by clicking the snapshot.

The Nature Preserve

Join us for a journey through the World Wide Web!

Home   Cats' Corner   Birds' Nest   Nature Paradises

CHAPTER 3

Changing the Size of an Image

Would you like to change the size of your image? This chapter shows you how, including how to change the on-screen or print size, change the resolution, and crop an image.

CHANGE THE ON-SCREEN SIZE OF AN IMAGE

You can change the size at which an image is displayed on your computer monitor so that viewers can see the entire image.

CHANGE THE ON-SCREEN SIZE OF AN IMAGE

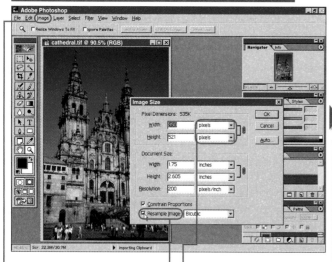

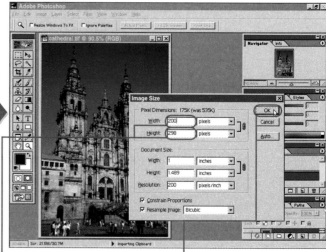

■1 Click **Image**.

■2 Click **Image Size**.

■ Photoshop displays the height and width of the image in pixels.

■ To resize by a certain percentage, click ▼ and change the units to **percent**.

■3 Make sure that **Resample Image** is checked (✓).

Note: Resampling is the process of increasing or decreasing the number of pixels in an image.

■4 Type a size for a dimension.

■ Because Constrain Proportions is checked, the other dimension changes proportionally.

■5 Click **OK**.

Note: You can restore the original dialog box settings by holding down Alt *(* Option *) and clicking the **Cancel** button, which changes to **Reset**.*

What is the difference between an image's on-screen size and its print size?

On-screen size depends only on the number of pixels that make up an image. Print size depends on the number of pixels as well as the print resolution (which is the density of the pixels on a printed page). Windows monitors display at 96 pixels per inch, so at that resolution on-screen size and print size are the same. (On a Macintosh, they are the same at 72 pixels per inch.) Higher resolutions print a smaller image, while smaller resolutions print a larger image.

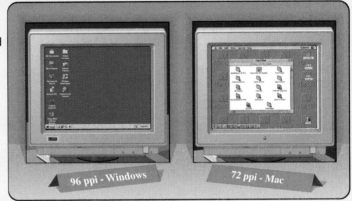

96 ppi - Windows

72 ppi - Mac

■ Photoshop resizes the image.

■ Changing the number of pixels in an image can add blur. To sharpen a resized image, apply the Unsharp Mask filter (see Chapter 11).

Note: You lose less detail when you decrease an image's size than when you increase it. So you are better off starting with an image that is too big than one that is too small.

■ This image was resized by setting the units to **percent** and typing **25** in the width and height fields. Photoshop decreased the image dimensions by three quarters.

CHANGE THE PRINT SIZE OF AN IMAGE

You can change
the printed size
of an image.

CHANGE THE PRINT SIZE OF AN IMAGE

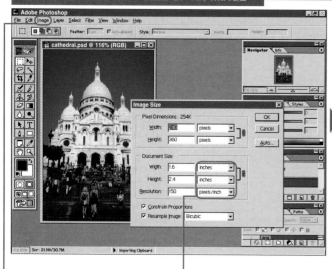

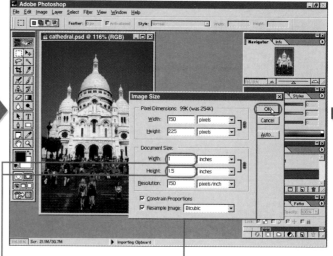

■1 Click **Image**.

■2 Click **Image Size**.

■ Photoshop displays the
current height and width of
the printed image.

■ You can click ▼ to change
the unit of measurement.

■3 Type a size for a
dimension.

■ The Constrain Proportions
setting changes the other
dimension proportionally.

■4 Click **OK**.

*Note: You can restore the original
dialog box settings by holding down*
Alt (Option) *and clicking* **Reset**.

How do I preview an image's printed size?

Click and hold the status bar of the application window (image window on the Macintosh). A diagram appears showing how the image will display on the printed page.

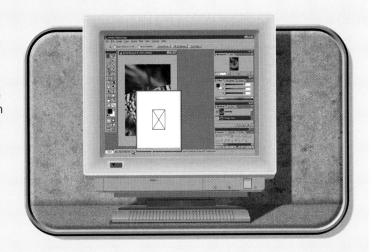

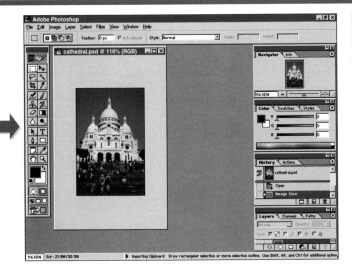

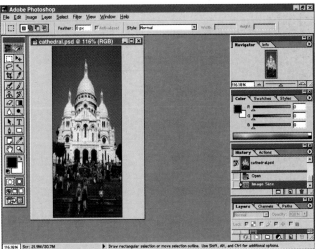

■ Photoshop resizes the image.

■ Changing the number of pixels in an image can add blur. To sharpen a resized image, apply the Unsharp Mask filter (see Chapter 11).

■ This image was resized with Constrain Proportions unchecked and the width changed. Photoshop decreases the width but not the height.

CHANGE THE RESOLUTION OF AN IMAGE

You can change the print resolution of an image to increase or decrease the print quality.

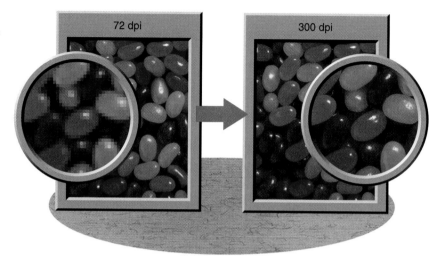

72 dpi

300 dpi

CHANGE THE RESOLUTION OF AN IMAGE

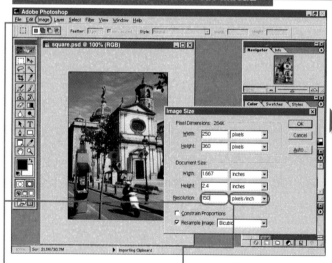

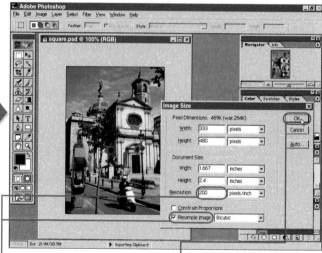

1 Click **Image**.

2 Click **Image Size**.

■ Photoshop displays the current resolution of the image. The resolution, combined with the number of pixels in an image, determines the size of a printed image.

■ You can click ▼ to change the resolution units.

Note: The greater the resolution is, the better the image will look on the printed page (up to a limit that varies with the type of printer).

3 Type a new resolution.

■ If Resample Image is checked, Photoshop adjusts the number of pixels in your image and keeps the printed dimensions fixed.

4 Click **OK**.

Note: You can restore the original dialog box settings by holding down Alt *(* Option *) and clicking* **Reset**.

What is the relationship between resolution, on-screen size, and print size?

To determine the printed size of a Photoshop image, you can divide the on-screen size by the resolution. If you have an image that is 480 pixels wide (its on-screen size) with a resolution of 120 pixels per inch, the printed width will be 4 inches.

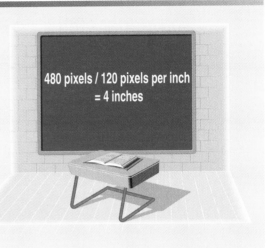

480 pixels / 120 pixels per inch
= 4 inches

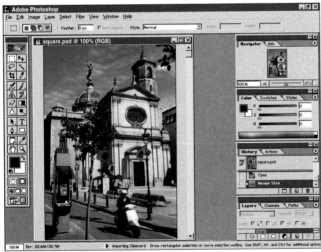

■ Modifying the resolution has changed the number of pixels in the image, so the on-screen image changes in size. (The print size stays the same.)

■ The resolution of this image was increased with resampling turned off. The on-screen image stays the same size. The printed size will be smaller.

CHANGE THE CANVAS SIZE OF AN IMAGE

You can change the canvas size of an image to change its rectangular shape or to add blank space to its sides.

The *canvas* is the area on which an image sits. Changing the canvas size is one way to crop an image.

CHANGE THE CANVAS SIZE OF AN IMAGE

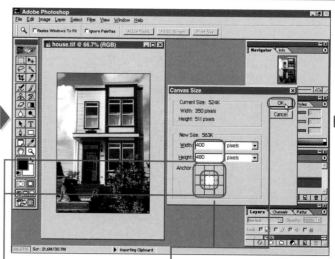

1 Click **Image**.

2 Click **Canvas Size**.

■ Photoshop displays the current dimensions of the canvas.

■ You can click 🔽 to change the unit of measurement.

3 Type the new canvas dimensions.

■ You can modify how Photoshop changes the canvas size by selecting an anchor point.

4 Click an anchor point (such as the middle one).

Note: The Crop tool (🔲) gives you an alternative to changing the canvas size (see the section "Crop an Image").

5 Click **OK**.

How does changing the canvas size affect the image size and resolution?

Changing the canvas size affects on-screen and print sizes but not image resolution.

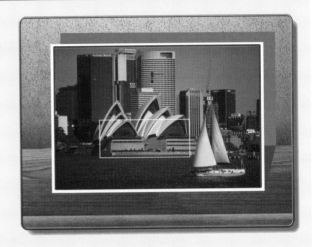

■ If you decrease a dimension, Photoshop displays a dialog box asking whether you want to proceed. Click **Proceed**.

■ Photoshop changes the image's canvas size.

■ Because the middle anchor point was selected in this example, the canvas changes equally on opposite sides.

■ Photoshop fills any new canvas space with the background color (in this case, white).

■ This canvas was resized by the same dimensions as the previous example but with the lower-left anchor point selected.

■ The canvas width changes only on the right side; the canvas height changes only on the top.

CROP AN IMAGE

You can use the Crop tool to change the size of an image.

CROP AN IMAGE

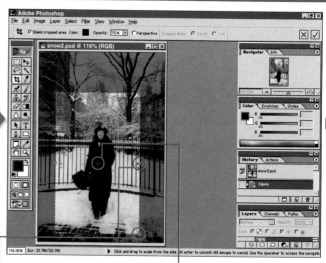

1 Click (the Crop tool).

2 Click and drag to select the area of the image you want to keep.

Note: You can also crop an image by changing its canvas size (see the section "Change the Canvas Size of an Image").

3 Click and drag the side and corner handles to adjust the size of the cropping boundary.

■ You can click and drag inside the cropping boundary to move it without adjusting its size.

4 Double-click inside the cropping boundary or press Enter.

Note: To exit the cropping process, you can press Esc (⌘ + .).

How do I increase the area of an image using the Crop tool?

Enlarge the image window to add extra space around the image. Then apply the Crop tool so that the cropping boundary extends beyond the borders of the image. When you apply cropping, the image canvas enlarges.

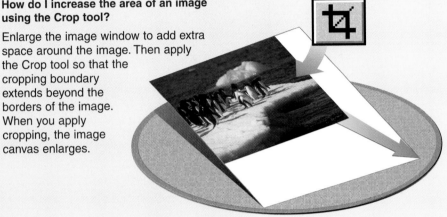

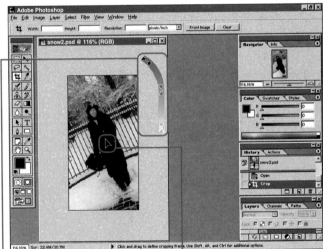

■ Photoshop crops the image, deleting the pixels outside of the cropping boundary.

ROTATE THE CROPPING AREA

1 Perform Steps 1 through 3 earlier in this section.

2 Click and drag outside of the boundary lines. Photoshop rotates the cropping boundary.

3 Double-click inside the cropping boundary.

DETERMINE THE SAVED FILE SIZE OF AN IMAGE

You can determine the
file size of an image
after you have saved it in
Photoshop.

DETERMINE FILE SIZE IN WINDOWS

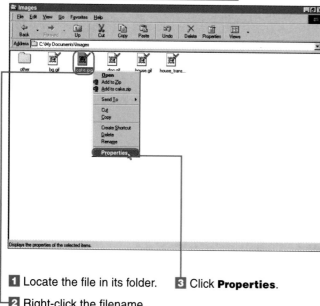

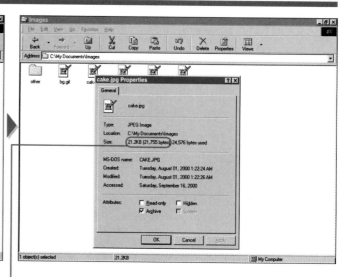

1 Locate the file in its folder.

2 Right-click the filename.

3 Click **Properties**.

■ A dialog box displays
information about the image,
including its file size.

*Note: There are 1,024 bytes in a
kilobyte (KB).*

What determines file size?

An image's file size depends on the number of pixels and colors it contains. For a given image, a bitmap version (which has just two colors) takes up less file space than a grayscale version (which has up to 256 shades of gray), and a grayscale version takes up less space than a color version (which can have millions of colors).

File size also varies with the file format. An image saved in an uncompressed format such as TIFF or BMP takes up more space than one saved in a compressed format such as JPEG or GIF. (See Chapter 14 for more on saving files as different formats.)

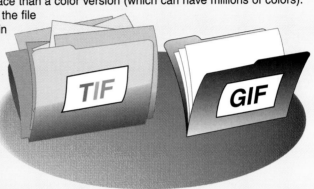

DETERMINE FILE SIZE ON A MACINTOSH

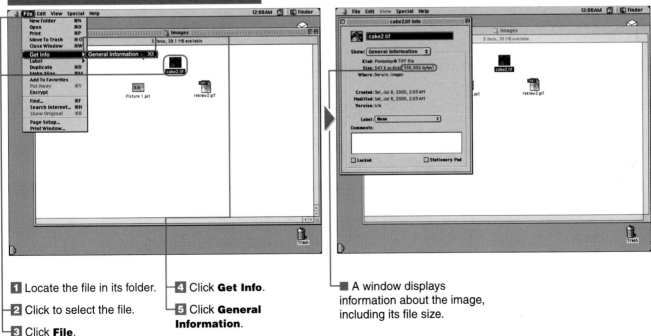

1 Locate the file in its folder.

2 Click to select the file.

3 Click **File**.

4 Click **Get Info**.

5 Click **General Information**.

■ A window displays information about the image, including its file size.

CHAPTER 4

Making Selections

Do you want to move, color, or transform elements of your image independently from the rest of the image? The first step is to select the object. This chapter shows you how.

SELECT WITH THE MARQUEE TOOLS

You can select a
rectangular or elliptical
area of your image by
using the Marquee tools.
Then you can move,
delete, or stylize the
selected area using other
Photoshop commands.

SELECT WITH THE RECTANGULAR MARQUEE TOOL

1 Click 🔲 (the Rectangular
Marquee tool).

2 Click and drag diagonally
inside the image window.

Note: You can hold down the **Shift**
*key while you click and drag to
create a square selection, or hold
down the* **Alt** *(* **Option** *) key to create
the selection from the center out.*

■ A rectangular portion of
your image is selected. Now
you can perform commands
on the selected area.

*Note: You can deselect a selection
by clicking* **Select** *and then*
Deselect.

How do I customize the Marquee tools?

You can customize the Marquee tool by using the boxes and menus in the Options bar. Entering a Feather value softens your selection edge (which means that pixels near the edge will be partially selected). The Style drop-down list lets you define your Marquee tool as a fixed size. You define the fixed dimensions in the Width and Height boxes.

SELECT WITH THE ELLIPTICAL MARQUEE TOOL

1 Click and hold ▣.

2 In the box that appears, click ◯ (the Elliptical Marquee tool).

3 Click and drag diagonally inside the image window.

Note: You can hold down the Shift *key while you click and drag to create a circular selection, or hold down the* Alt *(* Option *) key to create the selection from the center out.*

■ An elliptical portion of your image is selected. Now you can perform commands on the selected area.

SELECT ALL THE PIXELS IN AN IMAGE

You can select all the pixels in an image by using a single command. This lets you perform a subsequent command on the entire image, such as copying it to a different image window.

SELECT ALL THE PIXELS IN AN IMAGE

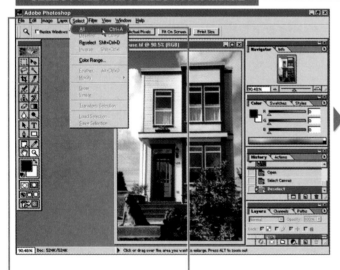

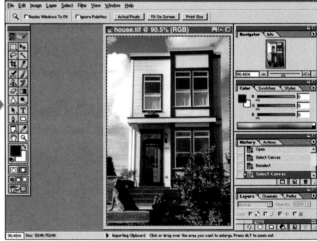

1 Click **Select**.

2 Click **All**.

■ The entire image window is selected.

Note: With the entire image window selected, you can easily delete your image (by pressing Delete *) or copy and paste it into another window.*

MOVE A SELECTION BORDER

You can move a
selection border if
your original selection
is not in the intended
place.

MOVE A SELECTION BORDER

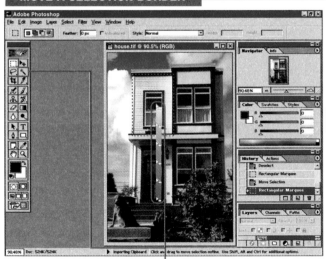

1 Make a selection with a
selection tool.

MOVE THE SELECTION BORDER

2 Click a selection tool (▣,
▨, or ▨).

3 Click and drag inside the
selection.

■ The selection border is
moved.

*Note: You can hide a selection by
clicking **View**, **Show**, and then
Selection Edges to uncheck the
menu option.*

SELECT WITH THE LASSO TOOL

You can create oddly shaped selections with the Lasso tool. Then you can move, delete, or stylize the selected area using other Photoshop commands.

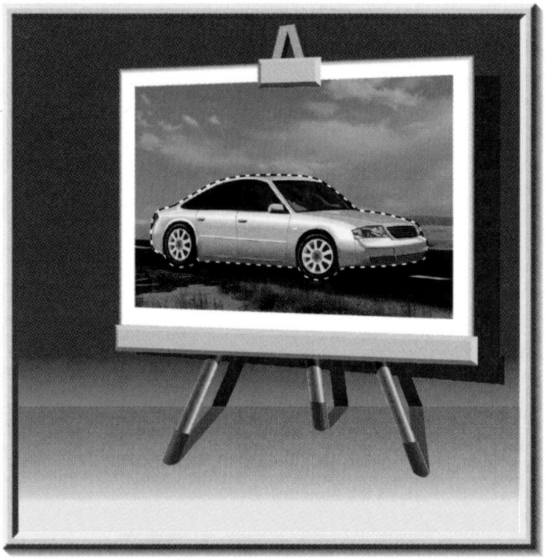

SELECT WITH THE LASSO TOOL

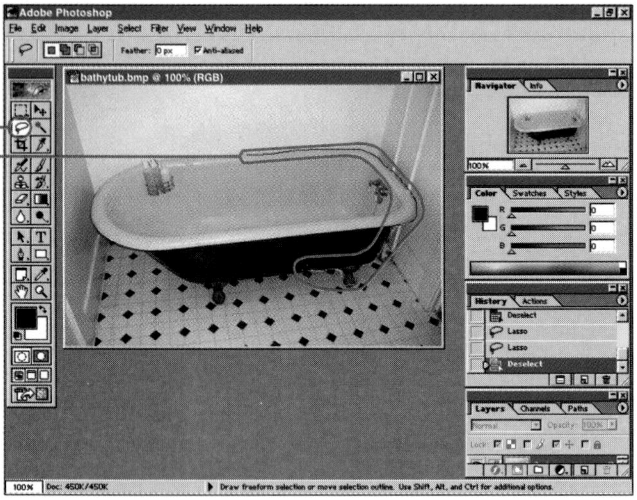

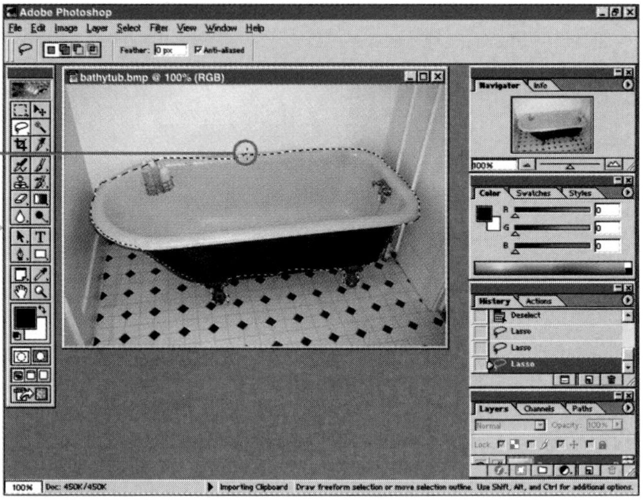

SELECT WITH THE REGULAR LASSO

1 Click (the Lasso tool).

2 Click and drag with your cursor to make a selection.

■ To accurately trace a complicated edge, you may want to magnify that part of the image with (see Chapter 2).

3 Drag to the beginning point and release the mouse button to complete the selection.

■ The selection is now complete.

What if my lasso selection is not as precise as I want it to be?

Selecting complicated outlines with the Lasso tool can be difficult, even for the steadiest of hands. To fix an imprecise Lasso selection, you can

- Deselect the selection (click **Select** and then **Deselect**) and try again.

- Try to fix your selection (see "Add to or Subtract from Your Selection").

- Switch to the magnetic lasso (see "Select with the Magnetic Lasso Tool").

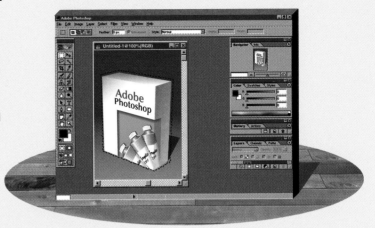

SELECT WITH THE POLYGONAL LASSO

Note: The Polygonal Lasso tool lets you easily create a selection made up of many straight lines.

1 Click and hold 🔲 and select 🔲 (the Polygonal Lasso tool) from the box that appears.

2 Click multiple times along the border of the area you would like to select.

3 To complete the selection, click the starting point.

Note: You can also double-click anywhere in the image and Photoshop will add a final straight line connected to the starting point.

■ The selection is now complete.

Note: You can get a polygonal effect with the regular Lasso tool by pressing **Alt** *(* **Option** *) and clicking to make your selection.*

SELECT WITH THE MAGNETIC LASSO TOOL

You can select elements of your image that have well-defined edges quickly and easily with the Magnetic Lasso tool.

SELECT WITH THE MAGNETIC LASSO TOOL

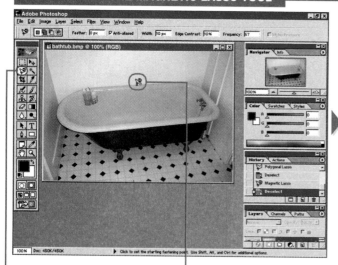

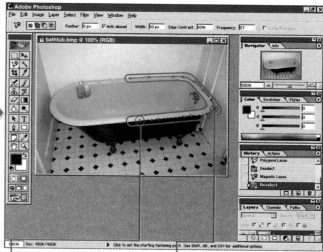

■1 Click and hold 🔲 and select 🔲 (the Magnetic Lasso tool) from the box that appears.

Note: The Magnetic Lasso works best when the element you are trying to select contrasts with its background.

■2 Click the edge of the element you want to select.

■ This creates a beginning anchor point.

■3 Drag your cursor along the edge of the element.

■ The Magnetic Lasso snaps to the edge of the element as you drag.

■ You can click to add anchor points as you go along. This helps guide the lasso.

How can I adjust the precision of the Magnetic Lasso tool?

You can use the the Options bar to adjust the Magnetic Lasso tool's precision:

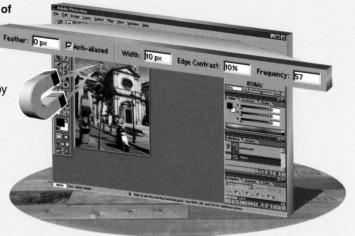

- **Width:** The number of nearby pixels the lasso considers when creating a selection

- **Edge Contrast:** How much contrast is required for the lasso to consider something an edge

- **Frequency:** The frequency of the anchor points

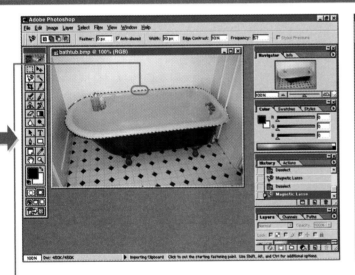

◢ Click on the beginning anchor point to finish your selection.

■ Alternatively, you can double-click anywhere in the image. Photoshop completes the selection for you.

■ The Magnetic Lasso is less useful for selecting areas of an image where there is little contrast.

SELECT WITH THE MAGIC WAND TOOL

You can select groups of similarly colored pixels with the Magic Wand tool.

SELECT WITH THE MAGIC WAND TOOL

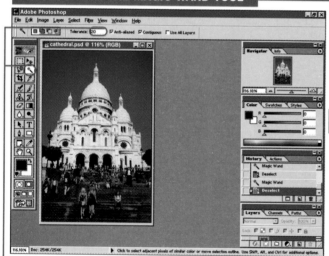

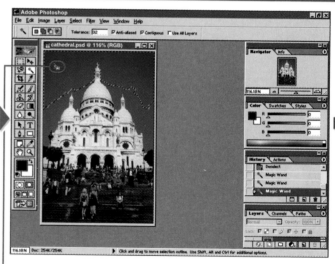

■1 Click ▦ (the Magic Wand tool).

■2 Type a number from 0 to 255 into the Tolerance field.

■ To select a narrow range of colors, type a small number; to select a wide range of colors, type a large number.

■3 Click on the area you want to select inside the image.

■ Photoshop selects the pixel you clicked, plus any similarly colored pixels near it.

With what type of images does the Magic Wand work best?

The Magic Wand tool works best with images that have areas of solid color. The Magic Wand tool is less helpful with images that contain subtle shifts in color or color gradients.

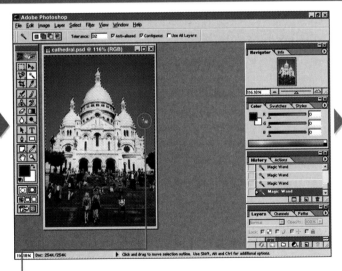

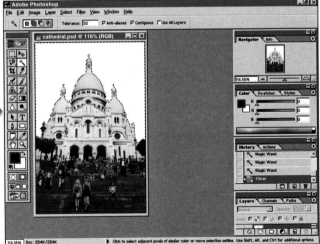

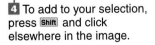

4 To add to your selection, press Shift and click elsewhere in the image.

■ Photoshop adds to your selection.

Note: The Magic Wand tool offers a quick way to separate an element from its background.

■ To delete the selected pixels, press Delete.

■ The pixels are replaced with the background color (in this case, white).

SELECT WITH THE COLOR RANGE COMMAND

You can select a set range of colors within an image with the Color Range command. This allows you to quickly select a region of relatively solid color, such as a sky or a blank wall.

SELECT WITH THE COLOR RANGE COMMAND

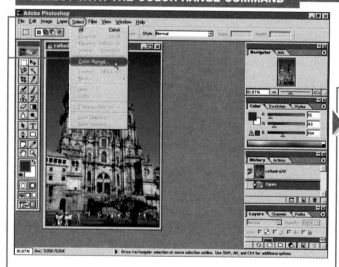

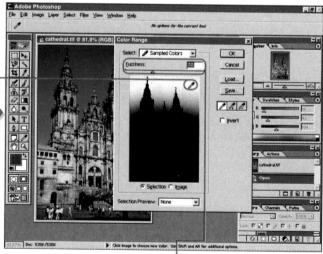

■1 Click **Select**.

■2 Click **Color Range**.

■ The Color Range dialog box appears.

■3 Click inside the image window.

■ Photoshop selects all the pixels in the image that are similar to the pixel you clicked. These areas turn white in the Color Range window.

■ The number of pixels that turn white depends on the Fuzziness setting.

How do I limit the area of the image affected by the Color Range?

Select an area of the image — by using the Marquee, Lasso, or other tool — before clicking **Select** and then **Color Range**.

4 To increase the range of color, move the Fuzziness slider to the right.

■ You can decrease the color range by moving the slider to the left.

■ You can also broaden the selected area by clicking the Add eyedropper (　) and then clicking other parts of the window.

5 Click **OK** to make a selection in the main image window.

■ Sometimes the Color Range command selects unwanted areas of the image. To eliminate these areas, see the section "Add to or Subtract from Your Selection."

ADD TO OR SUBTRACT FROM YOUR SELECTION

You can add to or
subtract from your
selection by using
various selection tools.

ADD TO A SELECTION

1 Make a selection using
one of Photoshop's selection
tools.

*Note: The selection in this example
was made using the Lasso tool (⊘).*

2 Click ⊘.

3 Click ▣ (the Add to
Selection button) in the
Options bar.

4 Select the area to be
added by using the Lasso
tool.

5 Complete the selection by
closing the Lasso path.

■ The original selection is
now enlarged.

■ You can enlarge the
selection further by
repeating Steps **2** through **5**.

*Note: You can also add to a selection
by pressing the* Shift *key as you
make your selection.*

What tools can I use to add to or subtract from a selection?

You can use any of the Marquee tools, any of the Lasso tools, or the Magic Wand tool to add to or subtract from a selection. All three have the Add to Selection and Subtract from Selection buttons available in the Options bar when they are selected.

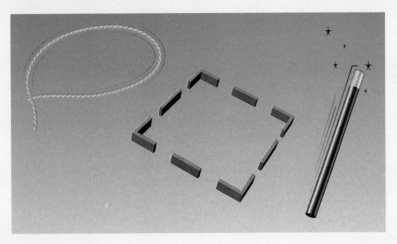

SUBTRACT FROM A SELECTION

▌1 Make a selection using one of Photoshop's selection tools.

Note: The selection in this example was made with the Rectangular Marquee tool (▣).

2 Click ▣.

3 Click ▣ (the Subtract from Selection button) in the Options bar.

▌4 Select the area to be subtracted.

■ Any part of the original selection that is part of the new selection is deselected (subtracted).

■ You can subtract other parts of the selection by repeating Steps 2 through 4.

Note: You can also subtract from a selection by holding down the **Alt** *(Option) key as you make your selection.*

EXPAND OR CONTRACT SELECTIONS

You can expand or contract a selection by a set number of pixels. This lets you easily fine-tune your selections.

EXPAND A SELECTION

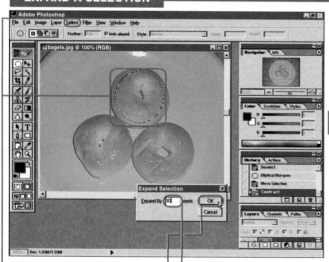

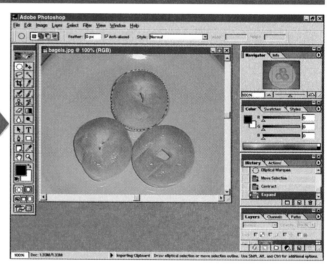

1 Make a selection using one of Photoshop's selection tools.

2 Click **Select**.

3 Click **Modify**.

4 Click **Expand**.

5 Type a value in the Expand By field.

6 Click **OK**.

Note: You can expand a selection up to 100 pixels at a time.

■ Photoshop expands the selection by the specified number of pixels.

■ You can repeat Steps **2** through **6** to expand a selection further.

How can I smooth the edges of a selection?

Make your selection and then click **Select**, **Modify**, and **Smooth**. Type a Sample Radius value. The greater the value, the more the selection will be smoothed.

CONTRACT A SELECTION

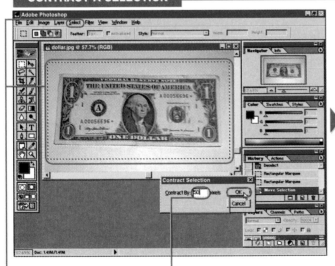

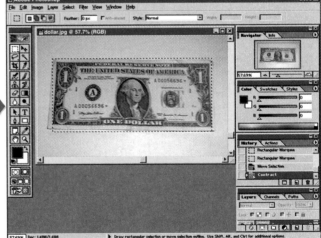

■1 Make a selection using one of Photoshop's selection tools.

■2 Click **Select**.

■3 Click **Modify**.

■4 Click **Contract**.

■5 Type a value in the Contract By field.

■6 Click **OK**.

Note: You can contract a selection up to 100 pixels at a time.

■ Photoshop contracts the selection by the number of pixels specified.

■ You can repeat Steps **2** through **6** to contract a selection further.

USING THE GROW AND SIMILAR COMMANDS

You can increase the size of your selection using the Grow and Similar commands.

USING THE GROW COMMAND

1 Make a selection using one of Photoshop's selection tools.

2 Click **Select**.

3 Click **Grow**.

■ The selection expands to include other similarly colored pixels.

Note: The Grow command expands to include only those pixels that are contiguous to the current selection.

Note: The amount the selection expands depends on the Tolerance value displayed in the Options bar when the Magic Wand tool is active. See "Select with the Magic Wand Tool" for details.

How do I invert a selection?

Click **Select** and then **Invert**. This deselects your selection and selects everything else.

USING THE SIMILAR COMMAND

1 Make a selection using one of Photoshop's selection tools.

2 Click **Select**.

3 Click **Similar**.

■ The selection expands to include other similarly colored pixels.

Note: The Similar command expands to include pixels anywhere in the image that are of a similar color, not just pixels that are contiguous to the selection.

Note: The amount the selection expands depends on the Tolerance value displayed in the Options bar when the Magic Wand tool is active. See "Select with the Magic Wand Tool" for details.

CHAPTER 5

Manipulating Selections

Making a selection defines a specific area of your Photoshop image. This chapter shows you how to move, stretch, erase, and manipulate in many other ways what you have selected.

MOVE A SELECTION

You can move a selection by using the Move tool, which lets you rearrange elements of your image.

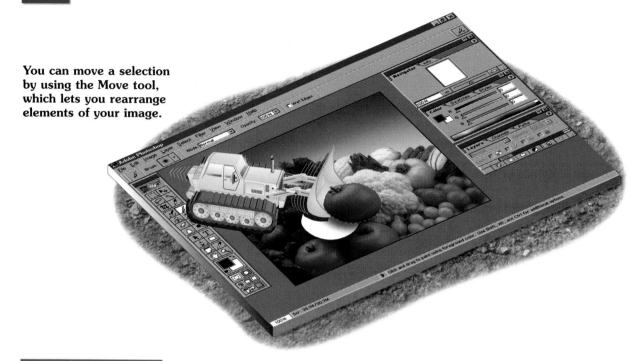

MOVE A SELECTION

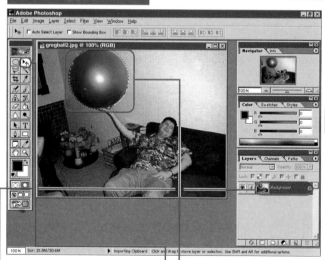

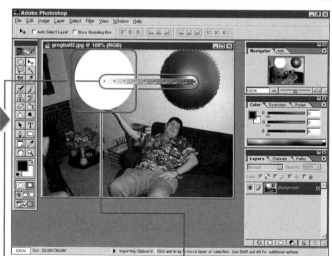

IN THE BACKGROUND

1 Click the Background layer in the Layers palette.

Note: If you are starting with a newly scanned image, the Background layer is probably your only layer.

2 Make a selection with a selection tool.

Note: See Chapter 4 for more on using selection tools.

3 Click the Move tool (⊕).

4 Click inside the selection and drag.

■ The area where the selection used to be fills with the current background color.

Note: White is the default background color.

How do I move a selection in a straight line?

Hold down the `Shift` key while you drag with the Move tool (⊞). Doing so constrains the movement of your selection horizontally, vertically, or diagonally (depending on the direction you drag).

IN A LAYER

Note: You can put elements of your Photoshop image in their own layers. For details about layers, see Chapter 9.

1 Click a layer in the Layers menu.

2 Make a selection with a selection tool.

Note: See Chapter 4 for more on using selection tools.

3 Click ⊞.

4 Click inside the selection and drag.

Note: Unlike the background (Photoshop's opaque default layer), layers can be transparent. This means that you can move elements in layers, and the areas they are moved from do not uncover the background color.

COPY AND PASTE A SELECTION

You can copy a selection and make a duplicate of it somewhere else in the image.

COPY AND PASTE A SELECTION

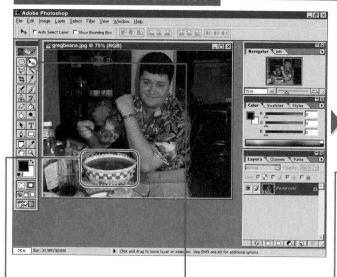

USING THE KEYBOARD AND MOUSE

1 Make a selection with a selection tool.

Note: See Chapter 4 for more on using selection tools.

2 Click ⊞.

3 Press Alt (Option) while you click and drag the selection.

4 Release the mouse button to "drop" the selection.

■ A duplicate of the selection is created and appears in the new location.

How can I copy a selection from one window to another?

Click 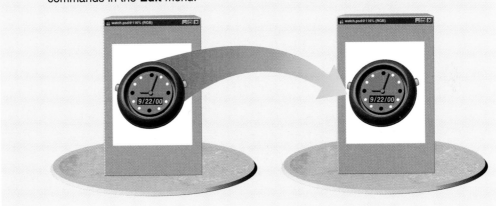, press **Alt** (**option**), and click and drag your selection from one window to another. You can also copy selections between windows using the **Copy** and **Paste** commands in the **Edit** menu.

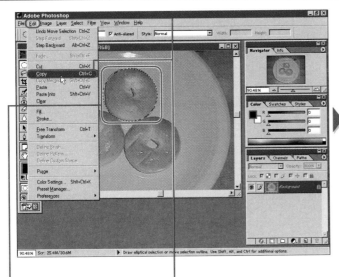

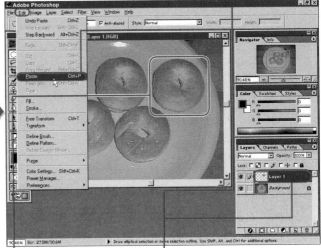

USING THE COPY AND PASTE COMMANDS

1 Make a selection with a selection tool.

Note: See Chapter 4 for more on using selection tools.

2 Click **Edit**.

3 Click **Copy**.

4 Using a selection tool, select the area where you want the copied element to be pasted.

■ If you do not select an area, Photoshop pastes the copy over the original.

5 Click **Edit**.

6 Click **Paste**.

■ Photoshop pastes the copy into a new layer. You can now move it independently of the original image (see "Move a Selection").

DELETE A SELECTION

You can delete a
selection to remove
elements from your
image.

DELETE A SELECTION

1 Make a selection with a
selection tool.

*Note: See Chapter 4 for more on
using selection tools.*

2 Press Delete.

■ The selection is deleted.

■ If you are working in the
background layer, the
empty selection fills with
the background color (in
this case, white, the default
background color).

■ If you are working in a
nonbackground layer,
deleting a selection turns
the selected pixels
transparent.

You can flip a selection
horizontally or vertically
to reverse the
orientation of an element
in your image.

FLIP A SELECTION

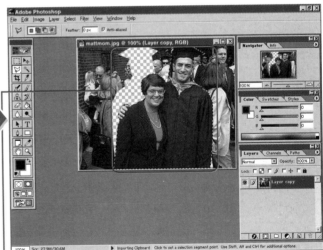

*Note: You can only flip selections
made in a nonbackground layer.*

1 Make a selection with a
selection tool.

2 Click **Edit**.

3 Click **Transform**.

4 Click **Flip Horizontal**.

■ You can click **Flip
Vertical** to flip the
selection vertically.

■ The selection is flipped,
becoming its mirror image.

■ In this example, the
empty space created by
flipping the layer is
transparent and is
represented by a
checkerboard pattern.

■ To flip an entire image,
you can click **Image**,
Rotate Canvas, and then
Flip Horizontal (or **Image**,
Rotate Canvas, and then
Flip Vertical).

ROTATE A SELECTION

You can rotate a
selection to tilt or turn
upside down an element
in your image.

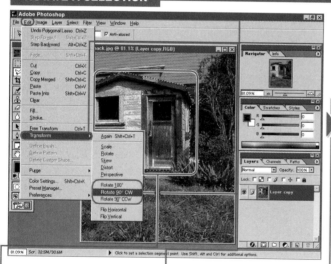

*Note: You can only rotate selections
made in a nonbackground layer.*

1 Make a selection with
a selection tool (see
Chapter 4).

2 Click **Edit**.

3 Click **Transform**.

4 Click a **Rotate**
command.

■ The selection rotates.

■ In this example, the
empty space created by
the rotation is transparent
and is represented by a
checkerboard pattern.

How can I rotate my entire image?

To rotate an entire image, click **Image**, **Rotate Canvas**, and then a **Rotate** command. If the image has multiple layers, this will rotate all of them the same amount.

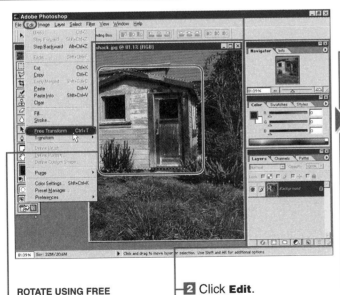

ROTATE USING FREE TRANSFORM

1 Make a selection with a selection tool (see Chapter 4).

2 Click **Edit**.

3 Click **Free Transform**.

4 Click and drag outside the bounding box to rotate the selection.

5 To apply the rotation, double-click inside the bounding box.

SCALE A SELECTION

You can scale a selection to make it larger or smaller.

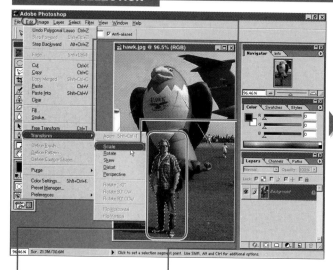

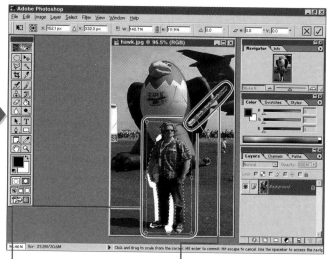

1 Make a selection with a selection tool.

Note: See Chapter 4 for more on using selection tools.

2 Click **Edit**.

3 Click **Transform**.

4 Click **Scale**.

■ A rectangular box with handles on the sides and corners surrounds the selection.

5 Click and drag a corner handle to scale both the horizontal and vertical axes.

**How do I scale both
dimensions
proportionally?**

Hold down the Shift
key while you scale
your selection. The two
axes of your selection
grow or shrink
proportionally. Your
image is not distorted.

⇧ Shift

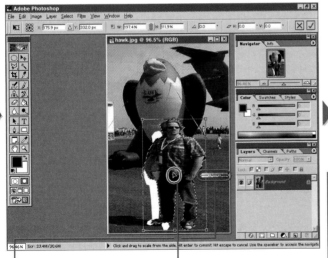

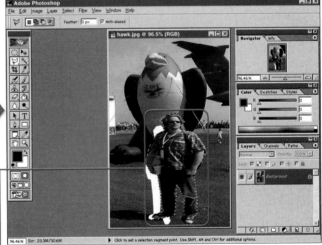

6 Click and drag a side
handle to scale one axis at
a time.

7 To apply the scaling,
double-click inside the
bounding box or press Enter
(Return).

■ To cancel the scaling,
you can press Esc
(⌘ + .).

■ The selection is scaled
to the new dimensions.

SKEW OR DISTORT A SELECTION

You can transform a
selection using the Skew
or Distort command.
This lets you stretch
elements in your image
into interesting shapes.

SKEW A SELECTION

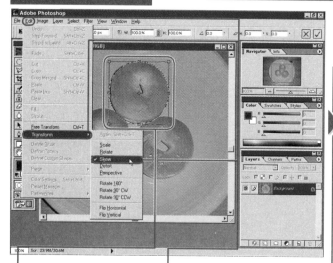

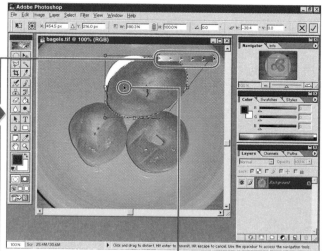

1 Make a selection with a
selection tool.

*Note: See Chapter 4 for more on
using selection tools.*

2 Click **Edit**.

3 Click **Transform**.

4 Click **Skew**.

■ A rectangular bounding
box with handles on the
sides and corners
surrounds the selection.

5 Click and drag a handle
to skew the selection.

*Note: The Skew command works
along a single axis; you can drag
either horizontally or vertically.*

6 Double-click inside the
bounding box to apply the
effect.

■ To cancel, you can press
`Esc` (⌘ + .).

How do I duplicate an item before skewing or distorting it?

Press Alt (option) while selecting the **Skew** or **Distort** command.

DISTORT A SELECTION

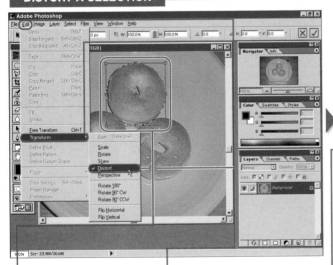

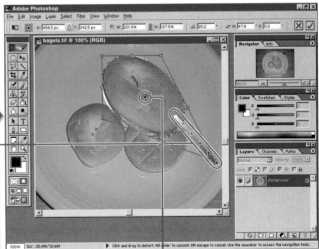

1 Make a selection with a selection tool.

Note: See Chapter 4 for more on using selection tools.

2 Click **Edit**.

3 Click **Transform**.

4 Click **Distort**.

■ A rectangular bounding box with handles on the sides and corners surrounds the selection.

5 Click and drag a handle to distort the selection.

Note: The Distort command works independently of the selection's different axes; you can drag a handle both vertically and horizontally.

6 Double-click inside the bounding box to apply the effect.

■ To cancel, you can press Esc (⌘ + .).

FEATHER THE BORDER OF A SELECTION

You can feather a selection's border to create soft edges.

FEATHER THE BORDER OF A SELECTION

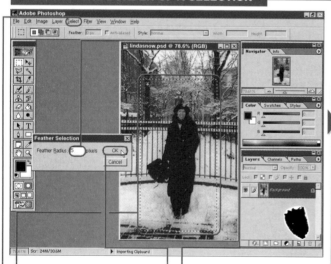

1 Make a selection with a selection tool.

Note: See Chapter 4 for more on using selection tools.

2 Click **Select**.

3 Click **Feather**.

4 Type a pixel value to determine the softness of the edge.

5 Click **OK**.

6 To delete the part of the image that surrounds your selection, first click **Select**.

7 Click **Inverse**.

■ The selection is inverted (but still feathered).

What happens if I feather a selection and then apply a command to it?

The command is applied only partially to pixels near the edge of the selection.

8 Press Delete.

■ By deleting the surrounding pixels, you can see the effect of the feathering.

■ The image in this example was feathered with a larger pixel value (20 pixels).

Note: To automate this feathering effect, see "Create a Vignette Effect" in Chapter 13.

USING THE RUBBER STAMP TOOL

You can clean up small flaws or erase elements in your image with the Rubber Stamp tool. The tool copies information from one area of an image to another.

USING THE RUBBER STAMP TOOL

Note: Step 1 is optional. It lets you limit where the rubber stamp is applied.

1 Make a selection with a selection tool.

Note: See Chapter 4 for more on using selection tools.

2 Click the Rubber Stamp tool (🖋) in the toolbox.

3 Click the Brush 🔽.

4 Select a brush size and type.

5 Press Alt (Option) and click the area of the image that you would like to copy from.

■ In this example, an area of empty grass is being selected with the tool.

Note: This area does not have to be inside the current selection.

How can I make the rubber stamp's effects look seamless?

To erase elements from your image with the rubber stamp without leaving a trace, try the following:

- Clone between areas of similar color and texture.

- To apply the rubber stamp more subtly, lower its opacity.

- Use a soft-edged brush shape.

6 Click and drag inside the selection to apply the rubber stamp.

■ The area is copied to where you click and drag.

7 Click and drag repeatedly over the area to achieve the desired effect.

■ In this example, the image of the horse has been copied over by the grass selection.

USING THE ERASER TOOL

You can make parts of your image disappear with the Eraser tool, which turns pixels in your layers transparent. (The Eraser tool has no effect on an image's background layer.)

USING THE ERASER TOOL

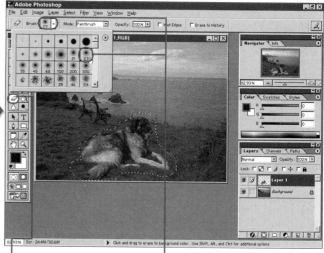

1 Click a layer.

Note: For more about layers, see Chapter 9.

■ If you want to limit where the eraser will be applied, you can make a selection with a selection tool (see Chapter 4).

2 Click the Eraser tool (🖉).

3 Click the Brush ▣.

4 Select a brush size and type.

How can I customize my eraser?

You can customize the eraser using settings in the Options bar. Adjustable settings include the following:

- The pencil or block option in the Mode list gives you a hard-edged brush.

- Lowering the Opacity setting lets you partially erase pixels.

- The Wet Edges option generates a semitransparent, watercolor effect.

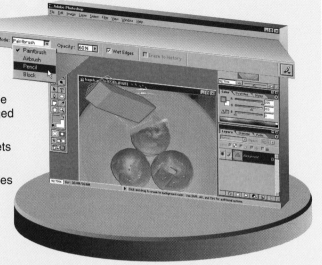

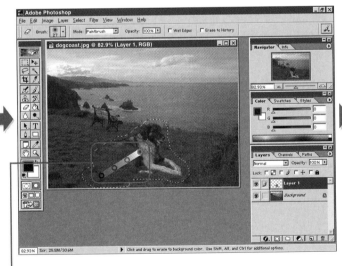

5 Click and drag inside the selection.

■ The tool turns areas of the layer transparent.

■ The tool has no effect on the background layer.

USING THE MAGIC ERASER TOOL

You can quickly turn large areas of a layer transparent with the Magic Eraser tool.

USING THE MAGIC ERASER TOOL

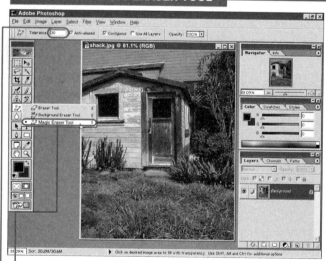

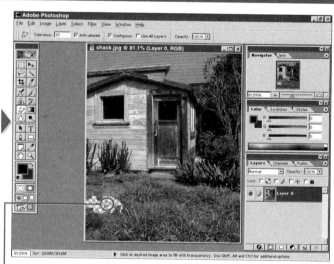

■1 Click and hold 🖉 and select the Magic Eraser tool (🖉) from the box that appears.

■2 Type a number from 0 to 255 into the Tolerance field.

■ To erase a narrow range of colors, type a small number; to erase a wide range of colors, type a large number.

■3 Click inside the image.

■ The pixel you click, plus any similarly colored pixels near it, turns transparent.

■ Photoshop represents transparency with a white-and-gray checker pattern.

**What is the Background
Eraser tool?**

The Background Eraser
tool ([🖉]), accessible by
clicking and holding [🖉] in
the toolbox, samples the
color from your image
where you first click it.
Then it erases similarly
colored pixels as you drag
it. This makes it useful for
erasing the solid
background around
elements in your image.

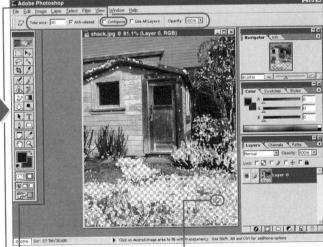

4 Click inside the image
again to delete more
pixels.

*Note: You can undo your eraser
commands by using the History
palette (see Chapter 2).*

■ You can adjust the tool
by using the settings in the
Options bar.

5 Click **Contiguous**
(☑ changes to ☐).

6 Click inside the image.

■ Pixels of a similar color,
but not necessarily
contiguous, to the one
being clicked are erased.

USING THE EXTRACT COMMAND

You can remove an element in an image from it's background using the Extract command.

USING THE EXTRACT COMMAND

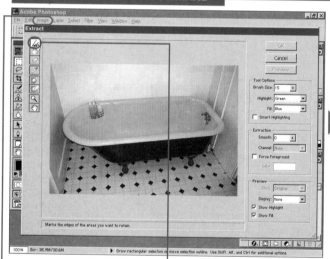

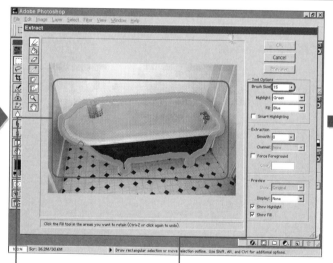

1 Click **Image**.

2 Click **Extract**.

■ Photoshop displays the image in the Extract dialog box.

■ If you make a selection before you perform the Extract command, only the selection will be displayed.

3 Click the Highlighter tool (🖉).

4 Highlight the edge of the element that you want to extract from the background.

■ The highlighting should overlay both the element and the background evenly.

■ You can change the size of the highlighter. For defined edges, use a smaller brush size; for fuzzier edges, use a larger brush size.

**My extraction has rough edges.
What can I do?**

You can improve a less-than-perfect extraction by clicking **Original** from the Extract dialog box's Show list. You can then edit your work. Click  to erase any errant highlighting, and then rehighlight those edges with the highlighting pen. (You can zoom in to trace the complicated parts.) Adjusting the Smooth slider can also help fine-tune the extraction process.

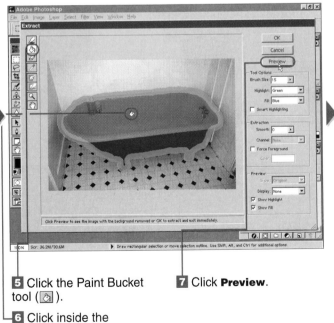

5 Click the Paint Bucket tool (🪣).

6 Click inside the highlighted element to fill it.

7 Click **Preview**.

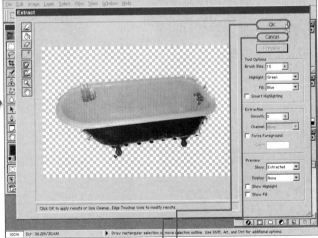

■ The element is extracted from the background.

8 Click **OK** to return to the original image window with the element extracted.

■ You can click **Cancel** to return without extracting.

CREATE SLICES

You can divide a large image that you want to display on the Web into smaller rectangular sections called *slices*. The different slices of an image can then be optimized independently of one another for faster download.

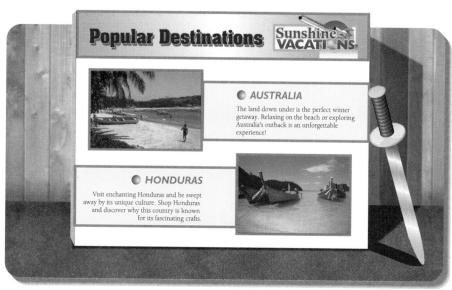

Slices can also be used to create special Web effects, such as animations and rollovers, in ImageReady. ImageReady is a Web imaging application that comes with Photoshop.

CREATE SLICES

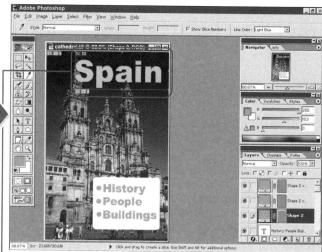

1 Click the Slice tool ().

2 Click and drag inside the image to create a slice.

■ Photoshop creates a slice where you clicked and dragged.

Note: Slices you define are called user-slices.

■ Photoshop fills in the rest of the image with auto-slices.

Note: User-slices remain fixed when you add more slices to your image, whereas auto-slices can change size.

How do I resize or delete slices in my image?

First, select the Slice Select tool (▼) (accessible by clicking and holding ✂). To resize a user-slice, click inside it and then click and drag a border handle. To delete a user-slice, click inside it and then press Delete .

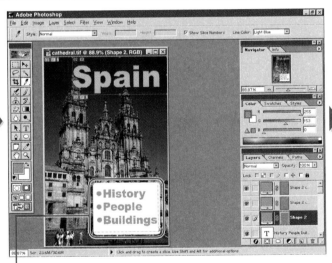

3 Click and drag to define another slice in your image.

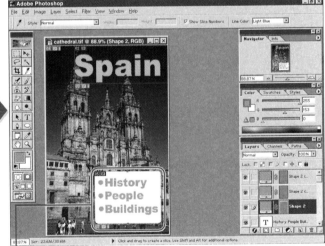

■ Photoshop creates another slice where you clicked and dragged.

■ Photoshop creates or rearranges auto-slices to fill in the rest of the image.

Note: To save the different slices, see Chapter 14.

Note: To learn about how to use slices in ImageReady, see Photoshop's Help information (see Chapter 1).

CHAPTER 6

Specifying Color Modes

Would you like to reduce the number of colors in your image or convert a color image to black and white? This chapter shows you how by specifying different color modes for your images.

WORK IN RGB MODE

You can work with a color image in RGB mode. RGB is the most common mode for working with color images in Photoshop.

RGB stands for Red, Green, Blue. In RGB mode, the image is stored as a combination of these three primary colors.

WORK IN RGB MODE

-■1 Click **Image**.

-■2 Click **Mode**.

-■3 Click **RGB Color**.

■ *RGB* is displayed in the image's title bar.

■ You can view the different color components of an RGB image with the Channels palette.

-■4 Click **Window**.

■5 Click **Show Channels**.

■6 Click the Red channel.

■ A grayscale version of the image displays the amount of red the image contains. Lighter areas mean lots of red; darker areas mean very little red.

What is CMYK mode?

Photoshop's CMYK mode represents an image's color information as a mix of cyan (C), magenta (M), yellow (Y), and black (K). You can use CMYK mode when your image needs to undergo color separation in preparation for offset printing.

7 Click the Green channel.

■ The amount of green in the image is displayed.

■ You can see the channel selection in the title bar.

8 Click the Blue channel.

■ The amount of blue in the image is displayed.

9 Click the RGB channel to return to the full-color image.

CONVERT COLOR IMAGES TO GRAYSCALE

You can remove the color from your image by converting it to grayscale mode. *Grayscale* images are made up of pixels that are white, gray, and black.

CONVERT COLOR IMAGES TO GRAYSCALE

1 Click **Image**.

2 Click **Mode**.

3 Click **Grayscale**.

■ Photoshop displays an alert box.

4 Click **OK**.

■ You can click the Don't Show Again check box (☐ changes to ☑) to avoid the alert in the future.

How do I make just part of my image grayscale?

Define the area you would like to turn gray with a selection tool and click **Image**, **Adjust**, and then **Desaturate**.

■ Every pixel in the image is converted to one of 256 shades of gray.

■ *Gray* is displayed in the image title bar.

5 Click **Window**.

6 Click **Show Channels**.

■ Grayscale images have a single channel (compared to an RGB image's three — see "Work in RGB Mode"), so grayscale image files take up less space than RGB images.

CREATE A DUOTONE

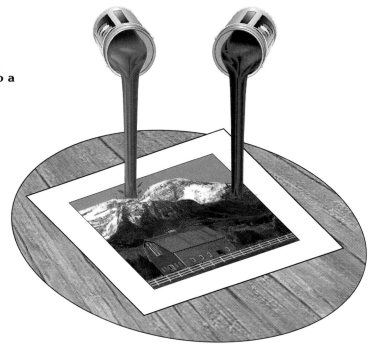

You can convert a
grayscale image to a
duotone.

A *duotone* is essentially a
grayscale image with a
color tint.

CREATE A DUOTONE

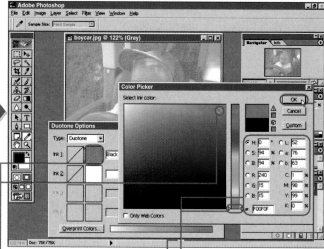

1 If necessary, convert
a color image to grayscale
(see "Convert Color Images
to Grayscale").

2 Click **Image**.

3 Click **Mode**.

4 Click **Duotone**.

5 Click ⬛ and click
Duotone.

6 Click the first color swatch
to open the Color Picker.

7 Click inside the window
to select your first duotone
color.

■ You can click and drag
the slider to change the color
selection. You can also enter
values in the boxes on the
right to define a precise
color.

8 Click **OK**.

How can I use duotones?

Duotones offer a quick and easy way to add color to a Web page or printed publication when all you have available are grayscale images.

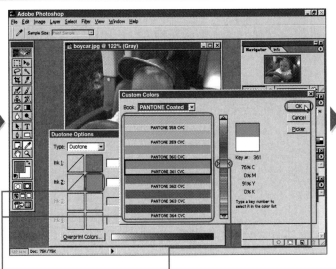

■9 Click the second color swatch to open the Custom Colors dialog box.

■10 Click inside the window to select your second duotone color.

■ You can click and drag the slider to change the color selection.

■11 Click **OK**.

■12 Click **OK** in the Duotone Options dialog box.

■ Photoshop uses the two selected colors to create the tones in the image.

CREATE A BITMAP IMAGE

You can convert a grayscale image to a bitmap image. In Photoshop, a bitmap image is made up of only black-and-white pixels.

The term *bitmap* is also used to describe any image made up of pixels. There is a file format called *bitmap* (abbreviated BMP) as well.

CREATE A BITMAP IMAGE

1 If you are working with a color image, convert it to grayscale (see "Convert Color Images to Grayscale").

2 Click **Image**.

3 Click **Mode**.

4 Click **Bitmap**.

5 Click ▼ and select an option for simulating the grayscale tones with black-and-white pixels.

6 Click **OK**.

How can I convert just part of my image to a bitmap?

Select an area of the image and click **Image**, **Adjust**, and then **Threshold**. The selected pixels will be converted to black and white. You can adjust the slider in the Threshold dialog box to achieve different effects.

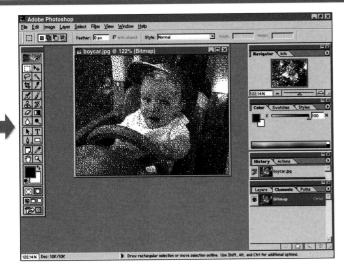

■ This figure shows the Diffusion Dither option, in which a random mixture of black-and-white pixels simulate the grayscale tones.

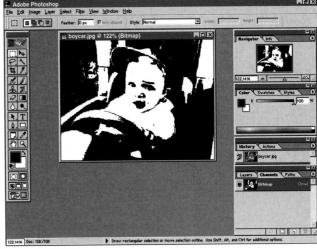

■ This figure shows the 50% Threshold option, in which pixels that are less than 50% black turn to white and pixels that are more than 50% black turn to black.

CREATE AN INDEXED COLOR IMAGE

You can reduce the number of colors that make up an image with the indexed color mode.

You can use the indexed color mode to prepare GIF images, which must contain 256 colors or fewer.

CREATE AN INDEXED COLOR IMAGE

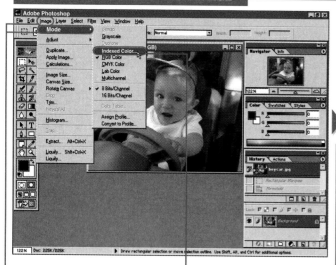

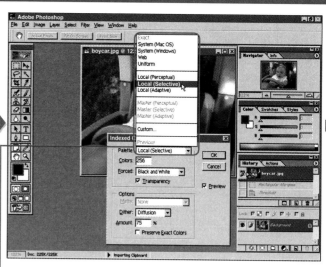

1 Click **Image**.

2 Click **Mode**.

3 Click **Indexed Color**.

■ The Indexed Color dialog box appears.

4 Click ▾ and select a color palette.

Note: The color palette you choose determines how Photoshop reduces the number of colors in the image.

Note: The Local (Perceptual), Local (Selective), and Local (Adaptive) palettes are similar in that they favor colors that are already present in the image.

Note: The Web and System palettes convert an image to "Web safe" and system colors, respectively.

What kind of images does the indexed color mode favor?

The indexed color mode works well with images that contain few colors, such as line drawings and flat-color illustrations. Converting these types of images to indexed color mode and saving them as GIFs can result in very small file sizes. Photographs usually do not fair well in indexed color mode because they usually require thousands or millions of colors to look good.

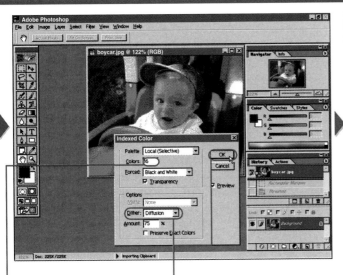

5 Select the number of colors your final image will contain.

Note: More colors will produce better-looking images, but fewer colors will result in a smaller file size.

6 Click ▾ and select a Dither option.

Note: With dithering turned on, Photoshop will mix two colors to simulate a third. This can help conserve colors and improve the quality of the indexed color image.

7 Click **OK**.

■ Photoshop reduces the number of colors in the image to the specified value.

CHAPTER 7

Painting with Color

Want to add splashes, streaks, or solid areas of color to your image? Photoshop offers a variety of tools with which you can add almost any color imaginable. This chapter introduces you to those tools and shows you how to choose your colors.

CHOOSE THE FOREGROUND AND BACKGROUND COLORS

You can select two colors to work with at a time in Photoshop — a foreground color and a background color. Painting tools such as the Paintbrush apply foreground color. You apply the background color when you use the Eraser tool, enlarge the image canvas, or cut pieces out of your image.

CHOOSE THE FOREGROUND AND BACKGROUND COLORS

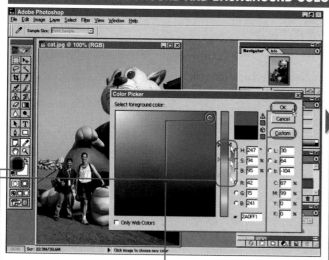

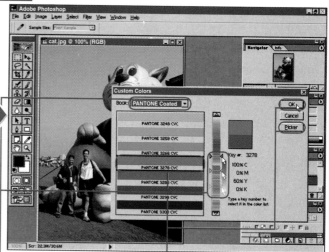

CHOOSE THE FOREGROUND COLOR

■1 Click the Foreground Color icon.

■2 To change the range of colors that appears in the window, click and drag the slider.

■3 To select a foreground color, click in the color window.

■4 Click **OK**.

■ Alternatively, you can click **Custom** to open the Custom Colors dialog box.

■ The Custom Colors dialog box enables you to choose colors from a set of predefined color libraries.

■5 Click ▼ and choose a book.

■6 To change the range of colors, click and drag the slider.

■7 Click a color to select it.

■8 Click **OK** to load your selection as the foreground color.

■ You can click **Picker** to return to the Color Picker.

How do I reset the foreground and background colors?

Click the Default icon to the lower left of the Foreground and Background icons. Doing so resets the colors to black and white.

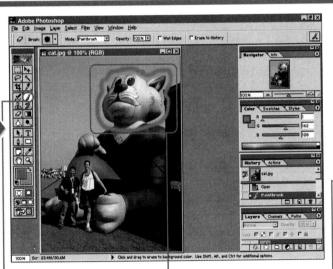

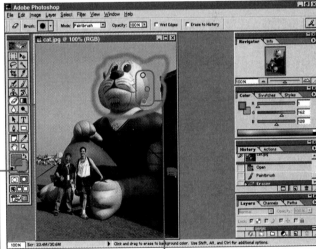

9 Click a painting tool in the toolbox (such as).

10 Click and drag to paint with the foreground color.

CHOOSE THE BACKGROUND COLOR

1 Click the Background Color icon.

2 Follow Steps **2** through **8** earlier in this section to select a background color.

3 Click .

4 Click and drag.

■ The tool "erases" by painting with the background color.

Note: This erasing occurs only in the background layer. In other layers, the eraser turns pixels transparent.

SELECT A COLOR WITH THE EYEDROPPER TOOL

You can select a color from an open image with the Eyedropper tool. The Eyedropper tool enables you to paint using a color already present in your image.

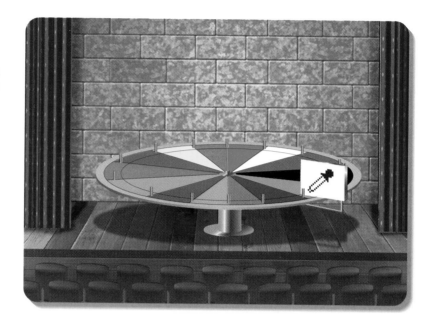

SELECT A COLOR WITH THE EYEDROPPER TOOL

■1 Click the Eyedropper tool ().

■2 Place ℐ over an open image.

■ If you click the Info palette tab, you can see color values as you move ℐ.

■3 Click to select the color of the pixel beneath ℐ's tip.

■ The color becomes the new foreground color.

Note: To select a new background color, you can press Alt *(* option *) as you click in Step 3.*

SELECT A COLOR WITH THE COLOR PALETTE

You can select a color with the color palette.

SELECT A COLOR WITH THE COLOR PALETTE

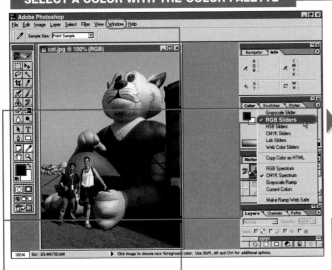

1 Click the Color palette (⊙).

2 Select a slider configuration from the Color palette menu.

■ If the Color palette is not visible, you can click **Window** and then **Show Color** to display it.

3 Click and drag the sliders to define the foreground color.

■ To define the background color, click the Background icon. To switch back, click the Foreground icon.

■ You can also select a color by clicking the color ramp. This can be faster than opening the Color Picker dialog box (see "Choose the Foreground and Background Colors").

USING THE SWATCHES PALETTE

You can select or store colors using the Swatches palette.

USING THE SWATCHES PALETTE

CHOOSE A COLOR

■1 Click **Window**.

■2 Click **Show Swatches**.

■ You can also click the Swatches tab.

■3 Click a color swatch to select a foreground color.

■ The color is stored as the foreground color.

■ To select a background color, press Alt (option) as you click in Step **3**.

STORE A NEW COLOR

■1 Click ✐.

■2 Click inside the image to select a color.

■3 Place ✐ over an empty area of the Swatches palette (✐ changes to 🖑).

■4 Click to add the color.

114

How can I create my own custom swatches?

Load your colors one by one into the Swatches palette, click the Swatches ⑨ , and then click **Save Swatches** in the Swatches palette menu. Swatches should be saved with an .aco file extension.

■ The Color Swatch Name dialog box appears.

5 Type a name for the new color swatch.

6 Click **OK**.

■ The color is added as a new swatch.

■ To remove a swatch, press Ctrl (⌘) and place ✐ over a swatch (✐ changes to ✂). Click to delete the swatch.

RESET THE SWATCHES PALETTE

1 Click the Swatches ⑨.

2 Click **Reset Swatches**.

SELECT A WEB-SAFE COLOR

You can select a Web-safe color in the color palette or color picker. Web-safe colors are important when creating images for display on Web pages. A Web-safe color is guaranteed to display accurately in all Web browsers, no matter what type of color monitor a user has.

See Chapter 14 for information about saving images with Web-safe colors.

SELECT A WEB-SAFE COLOR WITH THE COLOR PICKER

-■1 Click the Foreground icon.

■ The Color Picker window appears.

■2 Click **Only Web Colors** (☐ changes to ☑).

■ Photoshop displays only Web-safe colors in the Color Picker window.

-■3 Click a color.

■ The hex-code value for the selected color is displayed.

-■4 Click **OK**.

How do I load the Web-safe colors as a set of swatches?

Click **Window** and then **Show Swatches** to open the Swatches palette. Click the Swatches ⊙ and click **Web Safe Colors.aco**. The Web-safe colors are loaded into the Swatches palette.

SELECT A WEB-SAFE COLOR WITH THE COLOR PALETTE

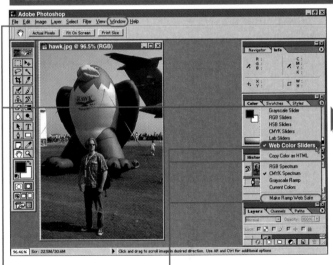

1 Click the Color ⊙.

■ If the Color palette is not visible, you can click **Window** and then **Show Color** to display it.

2 Click **Web Color Sliders**.

3 Click the Color ⊙ again.

4 Click **Make Ramp Web Safe**.

■ The Color palette sliders and color ramp now generate only Web-safe colors.

Note: To select a color, see "Select a Color with the Color Palette."

USING THE PAINTBRUSH TOOL

You can use the Paintbrush tool to add color to your image.

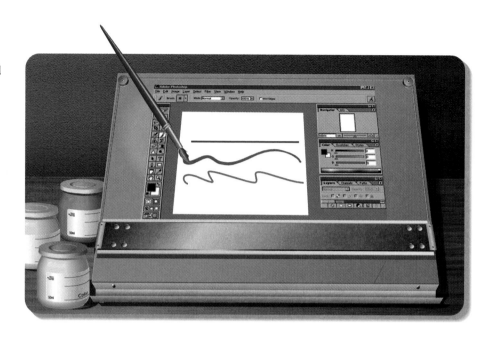

USING THE PAINTBRUSH TOOL

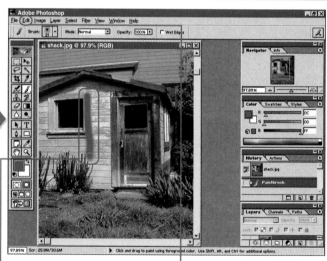

■1 Click the Paintbrush tool ().

■2 Click the Foreground icon to select a color to paint with.

Note: For details, see "Choose the Foreground and Background Colors."

■3 Click the Brush 🔽 and select a brush size and type.

■4 Click and drag to apply the foreground color to the image.

■ To undo the most recent brush stroke, click **Edit** and then **Undo Paintbrush**. To undo more than one brush stroke, use the History palette (see Chapter 2).

118

How do I paint thin lines?

Use the Pencil tool, which is similar to the Paintbrush tool except that it paints only thin, hard-edged lines. To select the Pencil tool, click and hold the Paintbrush tool and select the pencil from the box that appears.

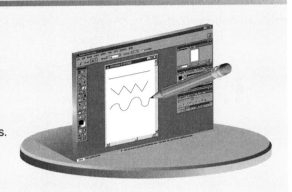

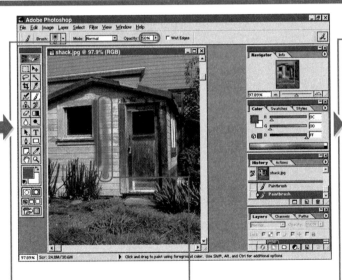

5 Type a percentage value to change the opacity of the brush strokes.

■ Alternatively, you can click the Opacity ▶ and adjust the slider.

6 Click and drag to apply the semitransparent paintbrush.

7 Click **Wet Edges** to concentrate the paint at the edges (☐ changes to ☑).

8 Click and drag to apply the customized paintbrush.

USING THE AIRBRUSH TOOL

You can use the Airbrush tool to add color to your image.

USING THE AIRBRUSH TOOL

1 Click the Airbrush tool (✍).

2 Click the Foreground icon to select a color.

Note: For details, see "Choose the Foreground and Background Colors."

3 Click the Brush ▯ and select a brush size and type.

4 Click and drag to apply the foreground color to the image.

■ To undo the most recent brush stroke, click **Edit** and then **Undo Airbrush**. To undo more than one brush stroke, use the History palette (see Chapter 2).

What happens when I click and hold with the Airbrush tool?

Doing so causes a constant stream of color to come out of the tool, enlarging the painted area. The Airbrush tool is the only painting tool whose effects change the longer you apply it one place.

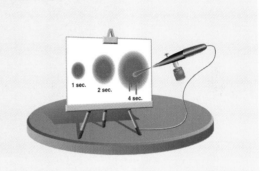

5 Type a percentage value in the Pressure field to change the opacity of the brush strokes.

■ Alternatively, you can click the Pressure ▶ and adjust the slider.

6 Click and drag to apply the semitransparent airbrush.

7 Click the Brush 🔽 and select a speckled brush type.

8 Click and drag to create a rougher effect.

CHANGE BRUSH STYLES

You can change the style of your brushes by loading premade styles or creating a custom style from scratch.

CHANGE BRUSH STYLES

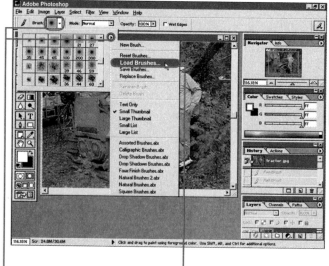

-1 Click the Brush ▣.

-2 Click ⊕.

-3 Click **Load Brushes**.

■ The Load dialog box appears.

-4 Click a brushes file.

-5 Click **Load**.

How can I make a brush apply dots instead of a line?

Click the brush style icon in the Options bar and increase the Spacing value to greater than 100%. When you click and drag, you get a discontiguous brush stroke.

6 Click the Brush ⬚.

7 Click a brush size and type.

Note: Loaded brush styles are listed after existing brush styles.

8 Click to apply the brush inside the image.

■ In this example, the brush was applied in single clicks (instead of clicking and dragging).

USING THE PAINT BUCKET TOOL

You can fill areas in your image with solid color using the Paint Bucket tool.

USING THE PAINT BUCKET TOOL

1 Click and hold the Gradient tool ( ).

2 Click the Paint Bucket tool ( ) in the window that appears.

3 Click the Foreground Color icon to select a color for painting.

Note: For details, see "Choose the Foreground and Background Colors."

4 Type a Tolerance value from 0 to 255.

Note: The Tolerance value determines what range of colors the paint bucket affects in the image when applied.

5 Click inside the image.

■ Photoshop fills an area of the image with the foreground color.

Note: The Paint Bucket tool affects adjacent pixels in the image.

**How can I reset a tool to the
default settings?**

Click on the tool's icon in the
Options bar and select **Reset
Tool**.

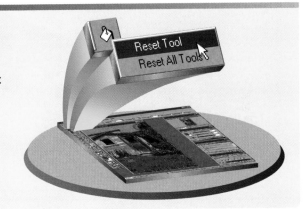

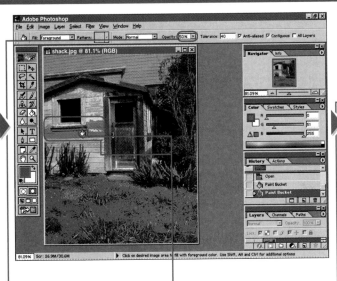

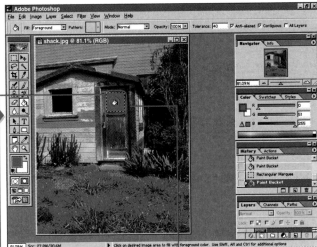

■6 To fill an area with a
semitransparent color, type
a percentage value of less
than 100 in the Opacity field.

■7 Click inside the image.

■ Photoshop fills an area
with see-through paint.

■8 To constrain where the
color is applied, make a
selection before clicking.

■ In this example, the
Opacity was reset to 100%.

■9 Click inside the selection.

■ The fill effect stays within
the boundary of the selection.

FILL A SELECTION

You can fill a selection with the Fill command. The Fill command is an alternative to the Paint Bucket tool (see "Using the Paint Bucket Tool").

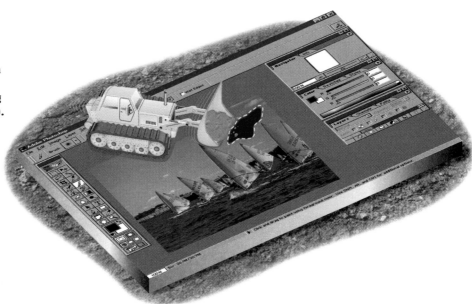

FILL A SELECTION

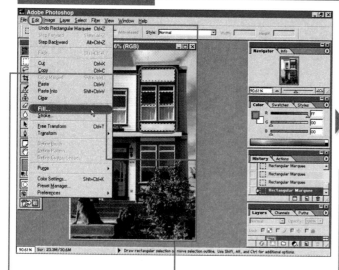

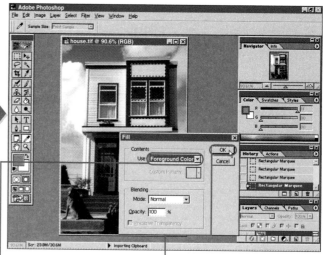

■1 Define the area you want to fill using a selection tool (see Chapter 4).

■2 Click **Edit**.

■3 Click **Fill**.

■4 Click the Use ▼ and select what you want to fill with.

■ To use the Pattern option, use [▢] to select an area of the image that you want to fill with. Next, click **Edit** and then **Define Pattern**.

■ The Saved option fills with content from the last saved version of the file.

■5 Click **OK**.

How do I apply a "ghosted" white layer over part of an image?

Use a selection tool to define the area of the image that you want to cover. Then apply the Fill command with White selected and the Opacity set to 50%.

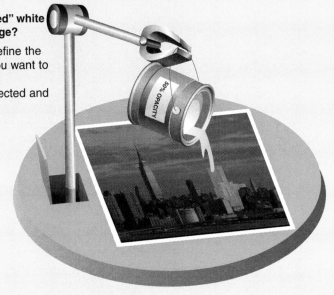

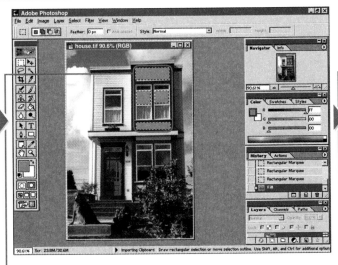

■ Photoshop fills the area.

■ The Fill command differs from the Paint Bucket tool (🔲) (see "Using the Paint Bucket Tool") in that it fills the entire selected area, not just adjacent pixels based on a tolerance value.

■ This is the Fill command performed with the background color instead.

DRAW SHAPES

You can create solid shapes in your image using Photoshop's many shape tools.

DRAW SHAPES

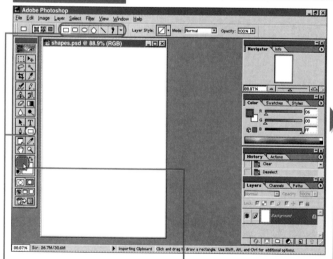

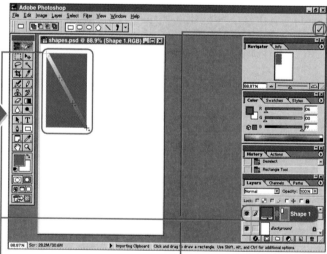

1 Click the Rectangle tool (□).

2 You can select other tools in the Options bar.

3 Click the Foreground Color icon to select a color for the shape.

Note: For details, see "Choose the Foreground and Background Colors."

4 Click and drag to draw the shape.

■ The shape appears in its own layer.

Note: For more information about layers, see Chapter 9.

■ You can click ☑ to redefine your shape tool.

How do I create straight lines?

Click the Line tool (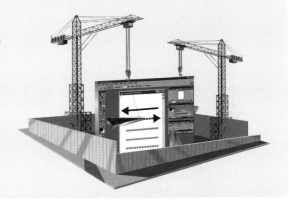), which is one of the shape tools. To add arrowheads to your lines, click the drop-down menu in the Options bar.

DRAW STYLED SHAPES

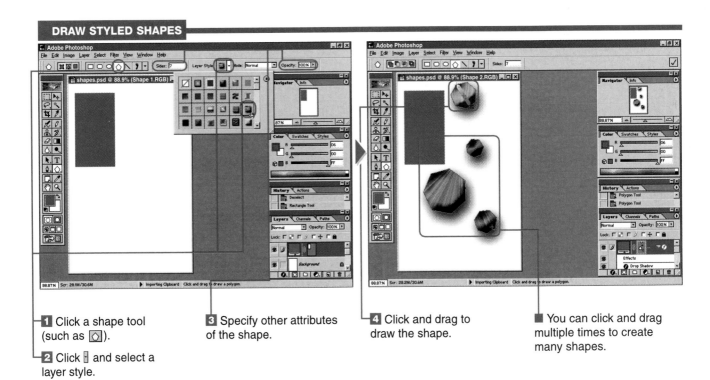

1 Click a shape tool (such as ⬡).

2 Click ▯ and select a layer style.

3 Specify other attributes of the shape.

4 Click and drag to draw the shape.

■ You can click and drag multiple times to create many shapes.

STROKE A SELECTION

You can use the Stroke command to draw a line along the edge of a selection.

STROKE A SELECTION

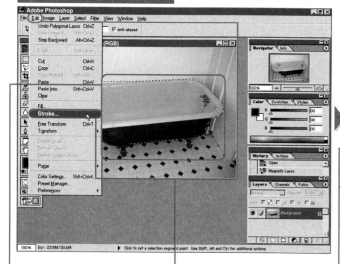

1 Select an area of the image with a selection tool (see Chapter 4).

2 Click **Edit**.

3 Click **Stroke**.

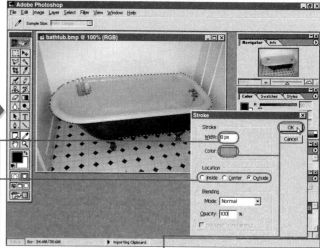

4 Type a width.

5 Click **Inside** to stroke a line on the inside of the selection, **Center** to stroke a line straddling the selection, or **Outside** to stroke a line on the outside of the selection (○ changes to ◉).

■ You can click the color swatch to define the color of the stroke.

6 Click **OK**.

How do I add a colored border to the outside of my image?

Click **Select** and then **All**. Then apply the Stroke command, clicking **Inside** as the Location. A border is added to the image.

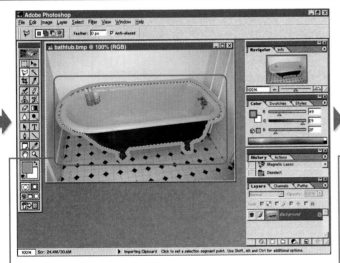

◾ Photoshop strokes a line along the selection.

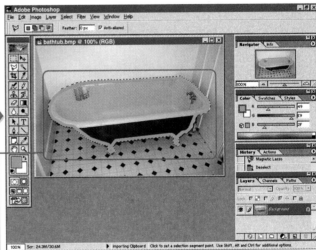

◾ This stroke was applied on the inside of the selection.

APPLY A GRADIENT

You can apply a
gradient, which is a
blend from one color to
another.

APPLY A GRADIENT

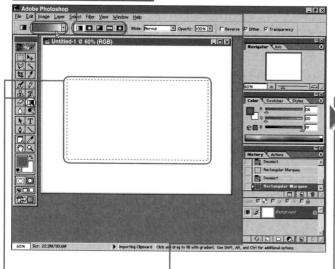

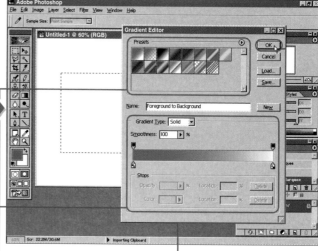

■1 Make a selection.

■ Your gradient will be
applied inside the selection.

■2 Click the Gradient
tool (□).

■ A linear gradient is
the default. You can select
different geometries in the
Options bar.

■3 Click the gradient swatch
to open the Gradient Editor.

■4 Select a preset gradient
type from the top window,
or define a custom gradient
using the settings below.

■5 Click **OK**.

**How can I add a rainbow gradient
to my image?**

Click a rainbow swatch in the
Gradient Editor. Doing so applies
the spectrum of colors from red to
violet. The radial gradient was
used here to put a rainbow burst
behind a layer containing a
person's head. (For more about
layers, see Chapter 9.)

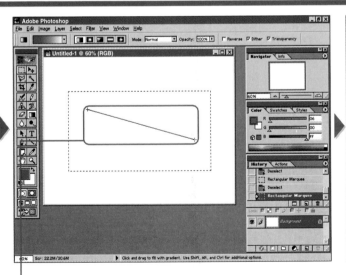

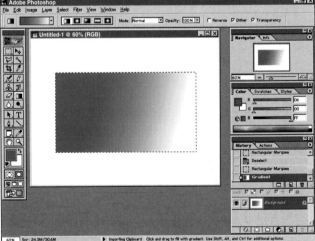

6 Click and drag inside
the selection.

*Note: This defines the direction and
transition of the gradient. Dragging
a long line with the tool produces a
gradual transition. Dragging a short
line with the tool produces an abrupt
transition.*

■ Photoshop generates a
gradient inside the selection.

USING THE HISTORY BRUSH

You can use the History brush to paint a previous state of your image from the History palette into the current image.

USING THE HISTORY BRUSH

1 Click the New Snapshot button (⬛) in the History palette.

■ Doing so puts a copy of the current state of the image into the History palette.

■ If the History palette is not visible, you can click **Window** and then **Show History** to display it.

2 Modify your image to make it different from the newly created snapshot.

3 Click to the left side of the snapshot to select it as the History brush source.

How do I paint a photograph onto a blank image with the History brush?

Start with a photographic image, take a snapshot of it, and then fill the image with a solid color. You can then use the History brush to paint in the photographic content.

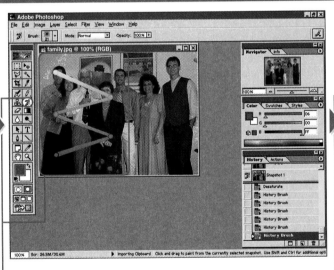

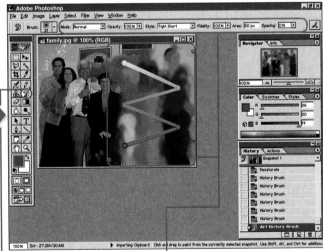

4 Click the History brush (▨).

5 Click and drag inside the image.

■ Pixel content from the previous snapshot is painted into the image.

6 Click and hold ▨ and select the Art History brush (▨).

7 Specify the settings for the brush.

8 Click and drag to apply an artistic effect.

CHAPTER 8

Adjusting Colors

Do you want to fine-tune the colors in your image — darken them, lighten them, or remove them completely? This chapter introduces the tools that do the trick.

CHANGE BRIGHTNESS AND CONTRAST

The Brightness/Contrast command provides a simple way to make adjustments to the highlights and shadows of your image.

CHANGE BRIGHTNESS AND CONTRAST

■1 Click **Image**.

2 Click **Adjust**.

3 Click **Brightness/Contrast**.

■ A dialog box opens with sliders set to 0.

4 To have your adjustments displayed in the image window as you make them, click **Preview** (☐ changes to ✓).

5 Click and drag the Brightness slider: Drag it to the right to lighten the image, or drag it to the left to darken the image.

■ You can also lighten the image by typing a number from 1 to 100 or darken the image by typing a negative number from -1 to -100.

How can I adjust the contrast of an image automatically?

Click **Image**, **Adjust**, and then **Auto Contrast**. Photoshop converts the very lightest pixels in the image to white and the very darkest pixels in the image to black. Making the highlights brighter and the shadows darker boosts the contrast, which can improve the appearance of some photographs.

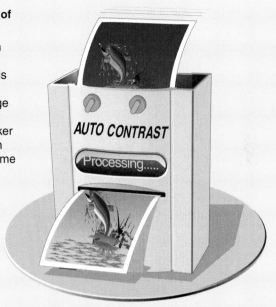

6 Click and drag the Contrast slider: Drag it to the right to increase the contrast, or drag it to the left to decrease the contrast.

■ You can also increase the contrast by typing a number from 1 to 100 or decrease the contrast by typing a negative number from -1 to -100.

7 Click **OK**.

■ The new brightness and contrast values are applied.

Note: If you make a selection before performing the Brightness/Contrast command, only the selected pixels are affected. Similarly, if your image is multilayered, only the selected layer is affected.

USING THE DODGE AND BURN TOOLS

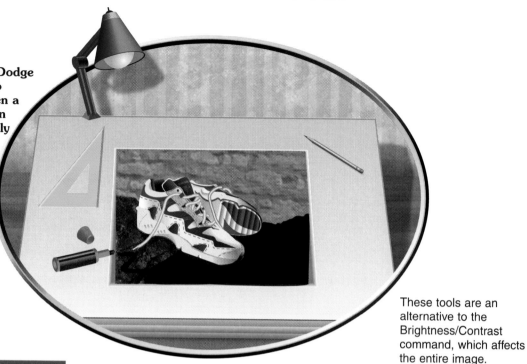

You can use the Dodge and Burn tools to brighten or darken a specific area of an image, respectively

These tools are an alternative to the Brightness/Contrast command, which affects the entire image.

USING THE DODGE TOOL

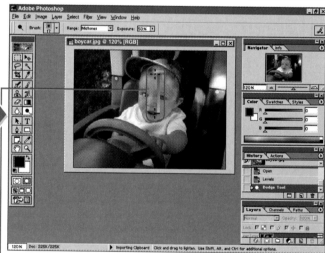

■1 Click 🔍 (the Dodge tool).

■2 Click the brush menu.

■3 Click the tool size that you would like to use.

■ You can also select the range of colors you want to affect and the tool's exposure (strength).

■4 Click and drag over the area that you want to lighten.

Note: Dodge is a photographic term that describes the diffusing of light when developing a film negative.

How do I invert the bright and dark colors in an image?

Click **Image**, **Adjust**, and then **Invert**. This makes the image look like a film negative. Bright colors become dark, and vice versa.

USING THE BURN TOOL

▉1 Click and hold 🔲.

▉2 Click 🔲 (the Burn tool) in the box that appears.

■ You can select the brush size, the range of colors you want to affect, and the tool's exposure (strength).

▉3 Click and drag over the area that you want to darken.

Note: Burn *is a photographic term that describes the focusing of light when developing a film negative.*

ADJUST LEVELS

The Levels commands lets you make fine adjustments to the highlights, midtones, or shadows of an image.

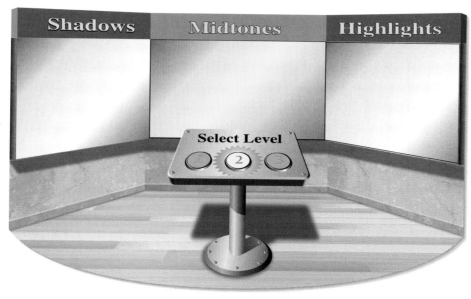

The Levels command offers more control over the brightness in an image than the Brightness/Contrast command does. But it is also more difficult to use.

ADJUST LEVELS

1 Click **Image**.

2 Click **Adjust**.

3 Click **Levels**.

■ The Input sliders let you adjust the brightness of the shadows (left), midtones (middle), and highlights (right).

4 To have your adjustments displayed in the image window as you make them, click **Preview** (☐ changes to ☑).

5 Click and drag the left slider to the right to darken the shadows in the image.

6 Click and drag the right slider to the left to lighten the bright areas of the image.

7 Click and drag the middle slider to adjust the midtones of the image.

Note: Performing Steps 5 and 6 has the effect of boosting the contrast in an image.

How do you adjust the brightness levels of an image automatically?

Click **Image**, **Adjust**, and then **Auto Levels**. Photoshop converts the very lightest pixels in the image to white and the very darkest pixels in the image to black. This command is similar to the Auto Contrast command (see "Change Brightness and Contrast") and can quickly improve the contrast of an overly gray photographic image.

Auto Levels

Processing.....

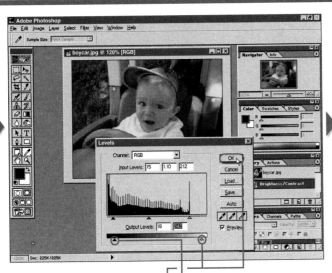

■ The Output sliders let you decrease the contrast while either lightening (using the left slider) or darkening (using the right slider) the image.

8 Click and drag the left slider to the right to darken the image.

9 Click and drag the right slider to the left to lighten the image.

10 Click **OK**.

■ Photoshop makes brightness and contrast adjustments to the image.

Note: If you make a selection before performing the Levels command, only the selected pixels are affected. Similarly, if your image is multilayered, only the selected layer is affected.

ADJUST HUE AND SATURATION

You can change the hue
to shift the component
colors of an image.
You can change the
saturation to adjust the
color intensity in an
image.

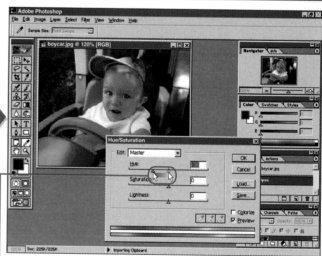

1 Click **Image**.

2 Click **Adjust**.

3 Click **Hue/Saturation**.

4 To have your adjustments
displayed in the image
window as you make them,
click **Preview** (☐ changes
to ☑).

5 Click and drag the Hue
slider to shift the colors in
the image. Dragging the
slider left or right shifts the
colors in different (and
sometimes bizarre) ways.

■ In this example, adjusting
the hue has changed the red
to magenta and the blue to
green.

How does the adjustment of an image's hues work?

When you adjust an image's hues in Photoshop, its colors are shifted according to their position on the color wheel. The color wheel is a graphical way of presenting all the colors in the visible spectrum.

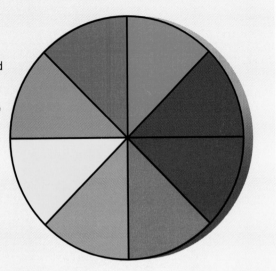

■6 Click and drag the Saturation slider to the right or to the left to increase or decrease the intensity of the image's colors, respectively.

■ If you check **Colorize**, Photoshop turns the image – even a grayscale one – into a monotone (one-color) image. You can adjust the color with the sliders.

■7 Click **OK**.

■ Photoshop makes the color adjustments to the image.

Note: If you make a selection before performing the Hue/Saturation command, only the selected pixels are affected. Similarly, if your image is multilayered, only the selected layer is affected.

USING THE SPONGE TOOL

You can use the Sponge tool to adjust the color saturation (color intensity) of a specific area of an image.

USING THE SPONGE TOOL

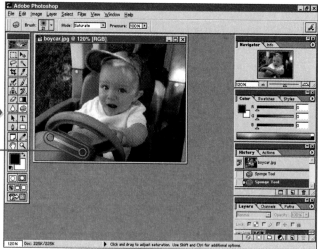

INCREASE SATURATION

1 Click and hold . Click (the Sponge tool) from the box that appears.

2 Click the brush menu.

3 Click the tool size that you would like to use.

4 Make sure that **Saturate** is selected.

5 Click and drag to increase the saturation of an area of the image.

How can I easily convert a color image to grayscale?

Click **Image**, **Adjust**, and then **Desaturate**. This command sets the saturation value of the image to 0, converting it to grayscale. This is an alternative to changing its mode (see Chapter 6).

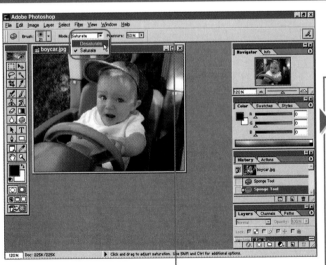

DECREASE SATURATION

1 Perform Steps 1 through 3 earlier in this section.

2 Click ⏷ and select **Desaturate**.

3 Click and drag to decrease the saturation of an area of the image.

■ You can adjust the strength of the Sponge tool by changing the Pressure setting (from 1% to 100%).

ADJUST COLOR BALANCE

You can use the Color Balance command to change the amounts of specific colors in your image.

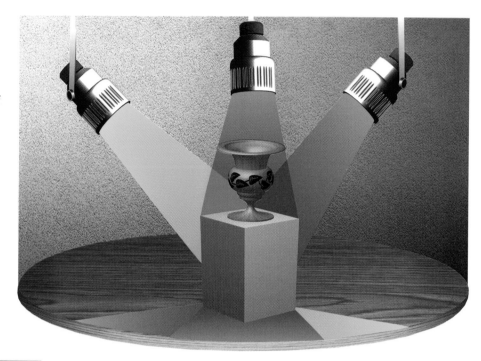

ADJUST COLOR BALANCE

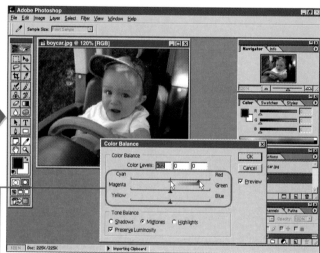

1 Click **Image**.

2 Click **Adjust**.

3 Click **Color Balance**.

4 To have your adjustments displayed in the image window as you make them, click **Preview** (□ changes to ☑).

5 Select the tones in the image that you want to affect (○ changes to ◉).

6 Click and drag a color slider toward the color you want to add more of.

■ To add a warm cast to your image, you can drag a slider toward red or magenta. To add a cool cast, you can drag a slider toward blue or cyan.

How do I change the color of an object in my image?

Select the object with a selection tool and then apply the Color Balance command.

7 Select another tonal range (○ changes to ◉).

8 Type a number from -100 to 100 in a color level field.

Note: Step 8 is an alternative to dragging a slider.

9 Click **OK**.

■ Photoshop makes color adjustments to the image.

Note: If you make a selection before performing the Color Balance command, only the selected pixels are affected. Similarly, if your image is multilayered, only the selected layer is affected.

USING THE VARIATIONS COMMAND

The Variations command gives you a user-friendly interface with which to perform color adjustments in your image.

USING THE VARIATIONS COMMAND

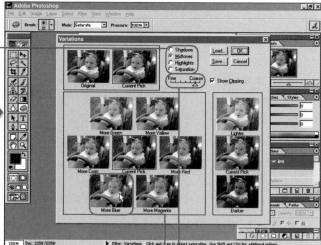

1 Click **Image**.

2 Click **Adjust**.

3 Click **Variations**.

4 Select a tonal range or **Saturation** (○ changes to ⦿).

*Note: Step 4 lets you apply effects to the different tones of your image. If you select **Saturation**, you can adjust just the image's saturation.*

5 Move the slider left to make fine (small) adjustments or right to make coarse (large) adjustments.

6 To add a color to your image, click one of the More thumbnails.

How can I undo color adjustments while using the Variations dialog box?

If you clicked one of the More thumbnail images to increase a color, you can click the More thumbnail image opposite to undo the effect. When added in equal amounts to an image, the colors opposite one another — for instance, red and cyan — cancel each other out. (Note that clicking the Original image in the upper-left corner returns the image to the state you started with as well.)

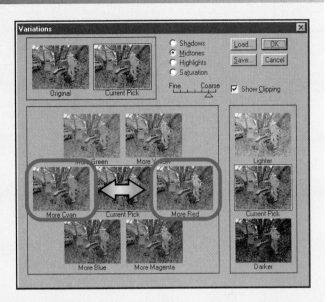

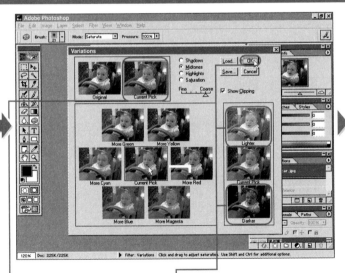

■ The result of the adjustment shows up in the Current Pick thumbnail.

■ To increase the effect, you can click the More thumbnail again.

7 To increase the brightness of the image, click **Lighter**.

■ You can decrease the brightness by clicking **Darker**.

8 Click **OK**.

■ Photoshop makes the color adjustments to the image.

Note: If you make a selection before performing the Variations command, only the selected pixels are affected. Similarly, if your image is multilayered, only the selected layer is affected.

APPLY THE BLUR AND SHARPEN TOOLS

You can sharpen or blur specific areas of your image with the Sharpen and Blur tools.

APPLY THE BLUR TOOL

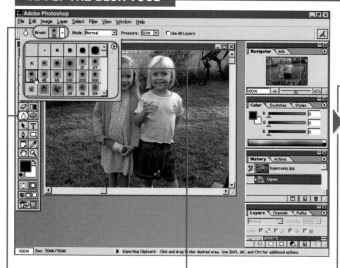

1 Click ◌ (the Blur tool).

2 Click the brush menu.

3 Click the tool size that you would like to use.

4 Click and drag to blur an area of the image.

Note: You can blur the entire image by using one of the Blur commands located in Photoshop's Filter menu (see Chapter 11).

What is the Smudge tool?

The Smudge tool () is another option located beneath the Blur tool (click and hold  to access it). It simulates dragging a finger through wet paint, shifting colors and blurring your image.

APPLY THE SHARPEN TOOL

1 Click and hold . Click  (the Sharpen tool) from the box that appears.

2 To change the pressure (strength) of the tool, enter a value from 1% to 100%.

3 Click and drag to sharpen an area of the image.

Note: You can sharpen the entire image by using one of the Sharpen commands located in Photoshop's Filter menu (see Chapter 11).

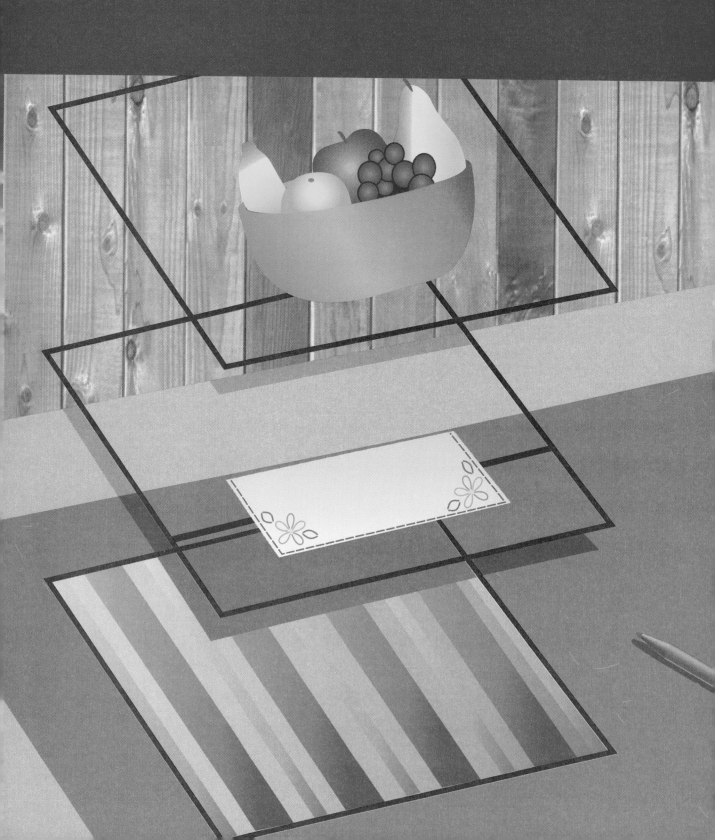

CHAPTER 9

Working with Layers

Do you want to separate the elements in your image such that you can move and transform them independently of one another? You can do this by putting them in different layers.

WHAT ARE LAYERS?

A Photoshop image can be made up of multiple layers, with each layer containing different elements of the image.

LAYER INDEPENDENCE

Layered Photoshop files act like several images combined into one. Each layer of an image has its own set of pixels that can be moved and transformed independently of the pixels in other layers.

APPLY COMMANDS TO LAYERS

Most Photoshop commands affect only the layer that is selected. For instance, if you click and drag using the Move tool, the selected layer will move while the other layers stay in place; if you apply a color adjustment, only colors in the selected layer will change.

MANIPULATE LAYERS

You can combine, duplicate, and hide layers in an image. You can also shuffle the order in which layers are stacked.

TRANSPARENCY

Layers can have transparent areas, where the elements on the layers below can show through. When you perform a cut or erase command on a layer, the affected pixels become transparent.

ADJUSTMENT LAYERS

Adjustment layers are special layers that contain information about color or tonal adjustments. An adjustment layer affects the pixels in all the layers below it. You can increase or decrease an adjustment layer's strength to get precisely the effect you want.

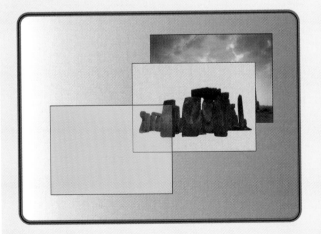

SAVE LAYERED FILES

Multilayered images can only be saved in the Photoshop file format. To save a layered image in another file format — for instance, PICT, TIFF, GIF, or JPEG — the image's layers must be combined into a single layer (a process known as *flattening*). For more information about saving files, see Chapter 14.

CREATE AND ADD TO A LAYER

To keep elements in your image independent from one another, you can create separate layers and add elements to them.

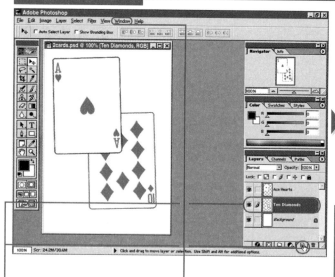

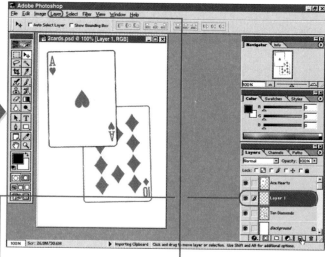

■1 Select the layer above which you want to add the new layer.

■2 In the Layers palette, click the New Layer button (🖻) (or click **Layer**, **New**, and then **Layer**).

■ If the Layers palette is not visible, you can click **Window** and then **Show Layers** to display it.

■ Photoshop creates a new, transparent layer.

■ You can rename the layer by clicking **Layer** and then **Layer Properties**.

158

What is the Background layer?

The Background layer is the default bottom layer that appears when you create a new image or when you import an image from a scanner. You can create new layers on top of a Background layer (but not below). Unlike other layers, a Background layer cannot contain transparent pixels.

ADD TO A LAYER

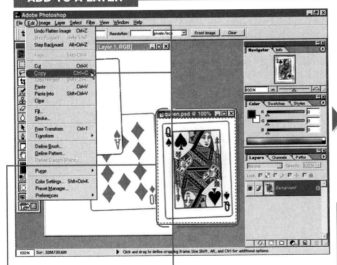

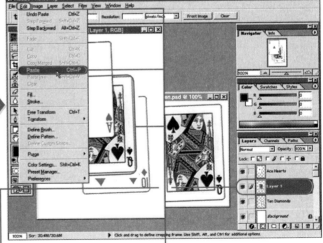

Note: This example shows adding content to the new layer by copying and pasting from another image file.

1 Open another image.

2 Using a selection tool, select the content you want to copy in the other image.

3 Click **Edit**.

4 Click **Copy**.

5 Click the image window where you created the new layer to select it.

6 Select the new layer in the Layers palette.

7 Click **Edit**.

8 Click **Paste**.

■ The content from the other image is pasted into the new layer.

HIDE A LAYER

You can hide a layer to temporarily remove elements in that layer from view.

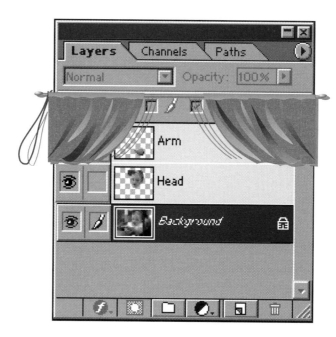

HIDE A LAYER

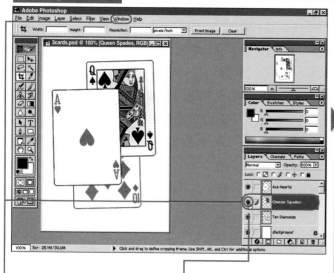

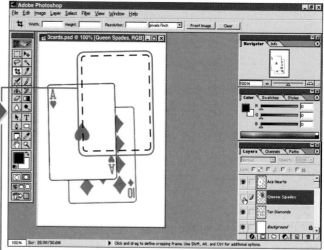

1 Select a layer.

■ If the Layers palette is not visible, you can click **Window** and then **Show Layers** to display it.

2 Click the 👁 for the layer.

■ Photoshop hides the layer.

Note: Hidden layers will not display when you print or use the Save for Web command.

■ To show one layer and hide all the others, you can **Alt** +click (Option +click) the 👁 for the layer.

Note: You can also delete a layer. See "Delete a Layer."

You can use the Move
tool to reposition the
elements in one layer
without moving those in
others.

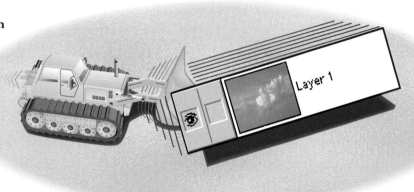

MOVE A LAYER

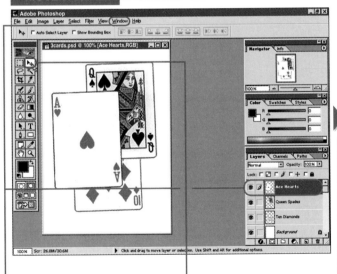

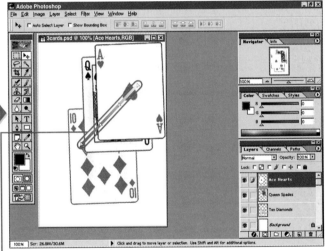

1 Select a layer.

■ If the Layers palette is not
visible, you can click **Window**
and then **Show Layers** to
display it.

2 Click the Move tool (⊕).

3 Click and drag inside the
window.

■ Content in the selected
layer moves. Content in the
other layers remains in the
same location.

*Note: To move several layers at
once, see "Link Layers."*

DUPLICATE A LAYER

By duplicating a layer, you can manipulate elements in an image while keeping a copy of their original state.

DUPLICATE A LAYER

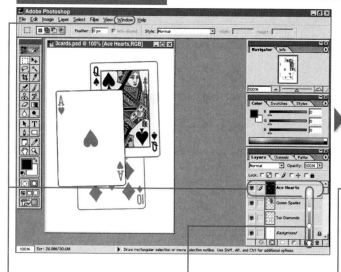

1 Select a layer.

■ If the Layers palette is not visible, you can click **Window** and then **Show Layers** to display it.

2 Click and drag the layer to ▣.

■ Alternatively, you can click **Layer** and then **Duplicate Layer**, in which case a dialog box will appear letting you name the layer.

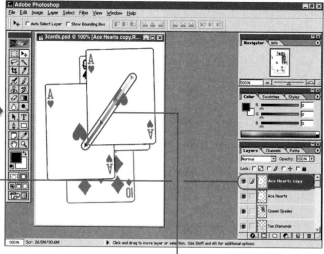

■ Photoshop duplicates the selected layer.

■ You can see that the layer has been duplicated by selecting the new layer, clicking ▣, and clicking and dragging.

You can delete a layer
when you no longer have
a use for its contents.

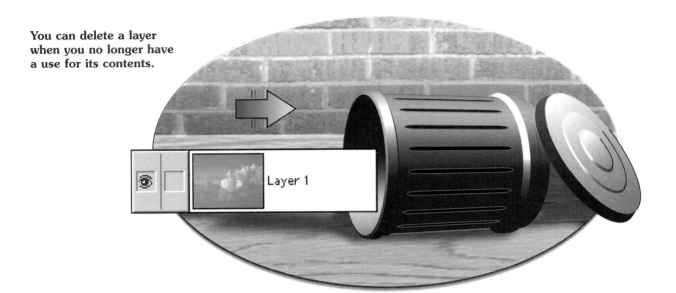

DELETE A LAYER

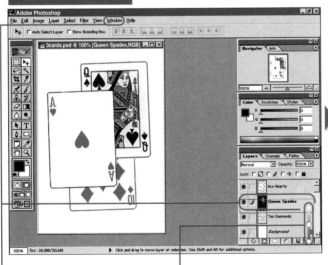

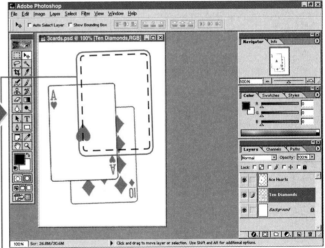

1 Select a layer.

■ If the Layers palette is not
visible, you can click **Window**
and then **Show Layers** to
display it.

2 Click and drag the layer
to 🗑.

■ Alternatively, you can click
Layer and then **Delete
Layer**, in which case a
confirmation dialog box will
appear.

■ Photoshop deletes the
selected layer. The content
in the layer disappears from
the image window.

REORDER LAYERS

You can change the stacking order of layers to move elements forward or backward in your image.

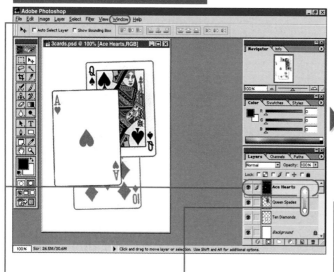

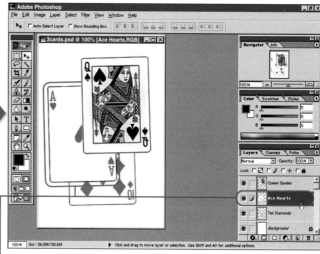

1 Select a layer.

■ If the Layers palette is not visible, you can click **Window** and then **Show Layers** to display it.

2 Click and drag the layer to change its arrangement in the stack.

■ The layer assumes its new position in the stack.

**Is there a shortcut for changing
the order of layers?**

You can shift a layer forward in the
stack by pressing `Ctrl` +] (`⌘` +]).
You can shift a layer backward by
pressing `Ctrl` + [(`⌘` +[).

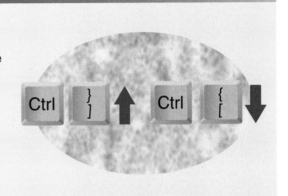

USING THE ARRANGE COMMANDS

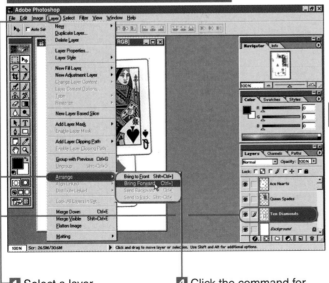

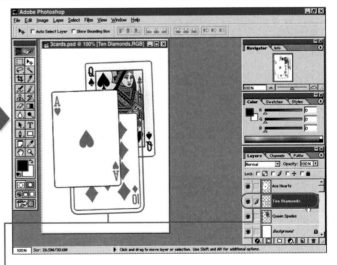

1 Select a layer.

2 Click **Layer**.

3 Click **Arrange**.

4 Click the command for
how you would like to move
the layer: **Bring to Front**,
Bring Forward, **Send
Backward**, or **Send to
Back**.

■ The layer assumes its
new position in the stack.

CHANGE THE OPACITY OF A LAYER

Adjusting the opacity of a
layer can let elements in
the layers below show
through. *Opacity* is the
opposite of transparency.
Decreasing the opacity of
a layer increases its
transparency.

CHANGE THE OPACITY OF A LAYER

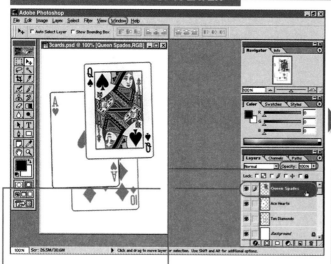

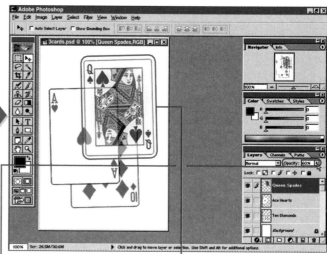

1 Select a layer other than
the Background layer.

*Note: You cannot change the opacity
of the Background layer.*

■ If the Layers palette is not
visible, you can click
Window and then **Show
Layers** to display it.

■ The default opacity is
100% (completely opaque).

2 Type a new value in the
Opacity field.

■ Alternatively, you can click
▶ and drag the slider.

*Note: A layer's opacity can range
from 1% to 100%. (To make a layer
completely transparent, see "Hide a
Layer.")*

■ The layer changes in
opacity.

How can I use changes in opacity in my images?

You can lower the opacity to add interesting type effects. For example, you can add a layer of semitransparent type over an image by reducing the type layer's opacity to 50%. (For more about adding type, see Chapter 12.)

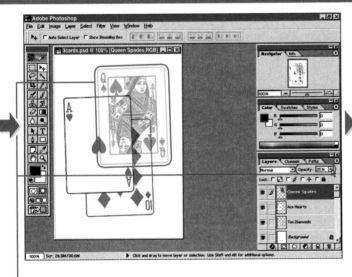

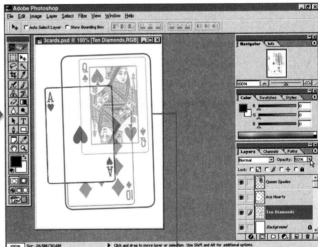

■ You can continue to adjust the opacity to suit your tastes.

■ You can make multiple layers in your image semitransparent by changing their opacities.

■ In this example, both the Queen Spades and Ten Diamonds layers are semitransparent.

MERGE AND FLATTEN LAYERS

Merging layers lets you permanently combine information from two or more separate layers. Flattening layers combines all the layers of an image into one.

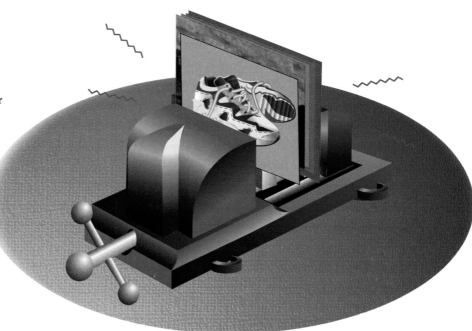

MERGE TWO LAYERS

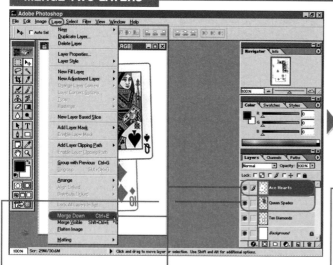

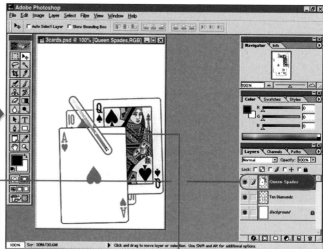

1 Arrange your layers so that the two layers you want to merge are next to one another (see "Reorder Layers").

■ If the Layers palette is not visible, you can click **Window** and then **Show Layers** to display it.

2 Select the topmost of the two layers.

3 Click **Layer**.

4 Click **Merge Down**.

■ The two layers are merged.

Note: The name of the lower layer is kept.

■ To see the result of the merge, select the new layer, click [+], and click and drag. The elements that were previously in separate layers now move together.

Why would I want to merge layers?

Merging layers enables you to save computer memory. The fewer layers a Photoshop image has, the less space it takes up in RAM and on your hard drive when you save it. Merging layers also lets you permanently combine elements of your image when you are happy with how they are arranged relative to one another. (If you want to be able to rearrange all the original layers in the future, save a copy of your image before you merge layers.)

FLATTEN AN IMAGE

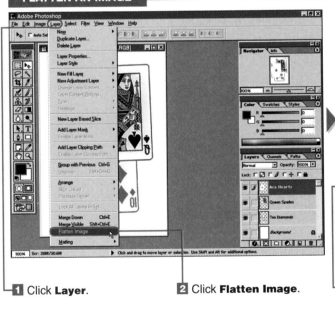

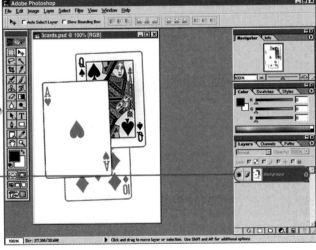

1 Click **Layer**.

2 Click **Flatten Image**.

■ All the layers are merged into one.

CREATE AN ADJUSTMENT LAYER

Adjustment layers let you store color and tonal changes in a layer, rather than having them permanently applied to your image.

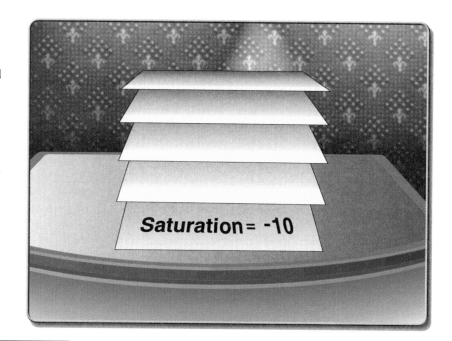

Saturation = -10

CREATE AN ADJUSTMENT LAYER

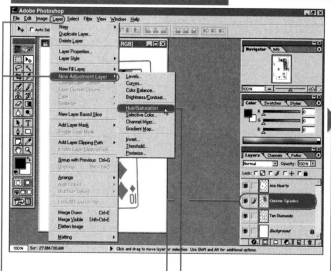

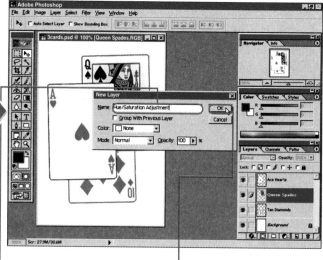

■1 Click **Layer**.

■2 Click **New Adjustment Layer**.

■3 Click an adjustment command.

Note: For more about these commands, see Chapter 8.

■ The new adjustment layer will be placed above the currently selected layer.

■4 Name the adjustment layer.

■5 Click **OK**.

How do I apply an adjustment layer to only part of my image canvas?

Make a selection with a selection tool before creating the adjustment layer.

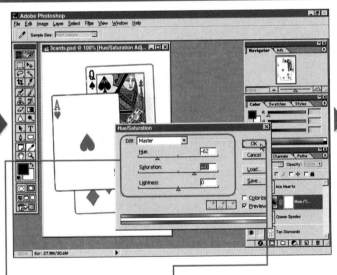

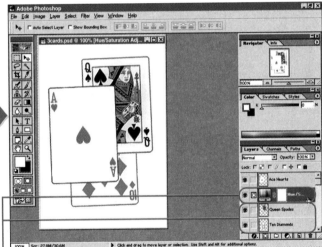

■ **6** Make your changes to the settings in the dialog box that appears.

■ In this example, an adjustment layer is created that changes the hue and saturation.

7 Click **OK**.

─■ An adjustment layer is added to the image.

─■ Photoshop applies the effect to the layers that are below the adjustment layer.

■ In this example, the card layers below the adjustment layer are affected while the card layer above is not.

You can change the color
and tonal changes that
you defined in an
adjustment layer.

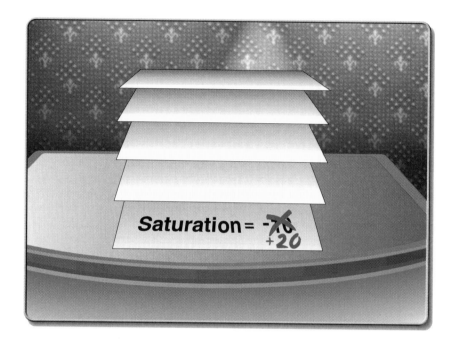

EDIT AN ADJUSTMENT LAYER

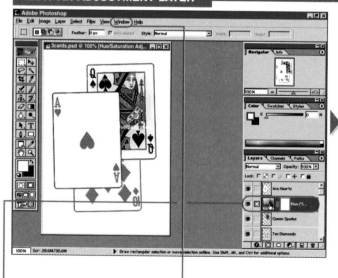

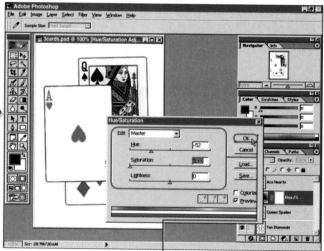

1 Double-click the
adjustment layer in the
Layers palette.

■ If the Layers palette is not
visible, you can click
Window and then **Show
Layers** to display it.

■ The Hue/Saturation dialog
box appears.

2 Make adjustments in the
dialog box.

3 Click **OK**.

How do I merge an adjustment layer with a regular layer?

Place the adjustment layer over the layer you would like to merge it with and then click **Layer** and **Merge Down**. Merging the layers will cause the adjustment layer's effects to be applied only to the layer it is merged with. The other layers below it will no longer be affected.

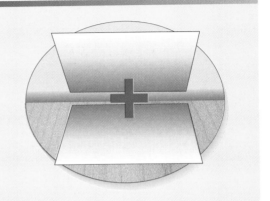

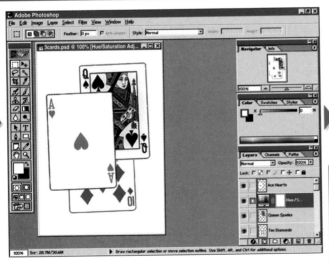

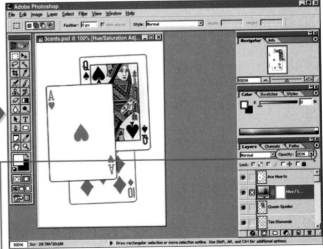

■ In this example, the saturation was reduced to the minimum, which removed the color in the layers below the adjustment layer.

◢4 To lessen the effect of an adjustment layer, decrease the layer's opacity to less than 100%.

■ In this example, the opacity was decreased to 20%, which reverses the decrease in saturation. Some of the original color in the cards returns.

LINK LAYERS

Linking causes different layers to move in unison when using the Move tool. Linking is useful when you want to keep elements of an image aligned with one another, but do not want to merge their layers (see "Merge and Flatten Layers"). Keeping layers unmerged lets you still apply effects independently to each.

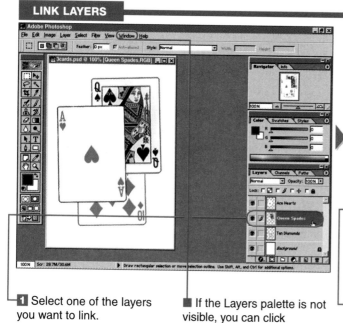

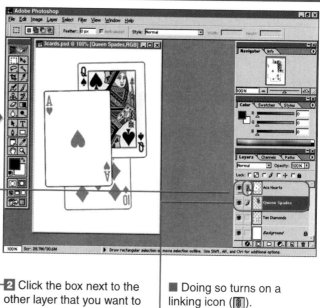

1 Select one of the layers you want to link.

■ If the Layers palette is not visible, you can click **Window** and then **Show Layers** to display it.

2 Click the box next to the other layer that you want to link.

■ Doing so turns on a linking icon (▒).

■ The layers link together.

How can I easily align content in several layers?

Link the layers you want to align and select one of the linked layers. Create a selection using the Marquee tool. Then click **Layer** and **Align to Selection** and choose an alignment. The menu lets you align the layers six different ways along the selection outline.

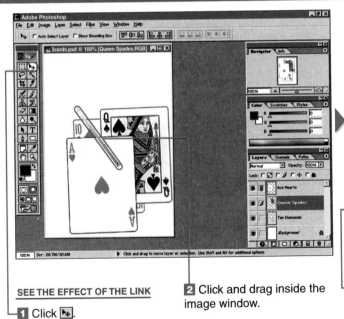

SEE THE EFFECT OF THE LINK

1 Click ⊕.

2 Click and drag inside the image window.

■ The linked layers move together.

■ You can link as many layers as you like.

■ In this example, all the layers have been linked, including the Background layer.

BLEND LAYERS

You can use Photoshop's blending modes to specify how pixels in a layer are blended with the layers below it.

BLEND LAYERS

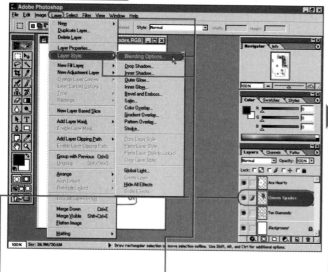

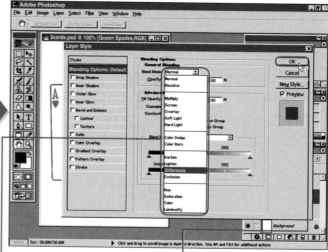

1 Select the layer that you want to blend.

■ If the Layers palette is not visible, you can click **Window** and then **Show Layers** to display it.

2 Click **Layer**.

3 Click **Layer Style**.

4 Click **Blending Options**.

5 Click the Blend Mode ▼ and select a mode.

6 Click **OK**.

**What effects do some of the
different blending modes have?**

The Multiply mode darkens the
colors where the selected layer
overlaps layers below it. The
Screen mode is the opposite of
Multiply; it lightens colors where
layers overlap. Color takes the
selected layer's colors and blends
them with the details in the layers
below it. Luminosity is the opposite
of Color; it takes the selected
layer's details and mixes them with
the colors below it.

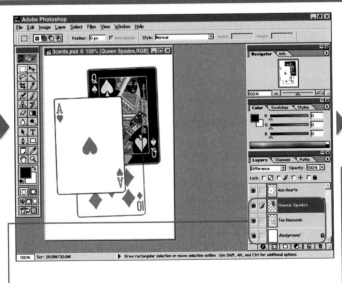

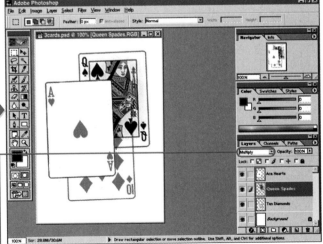

■ Photoshop blends the
selected layer with the layers
below it.

■ This example shows the
Difference mode, which
creates a photo-negative
effect in which the selected
layer overlaps other layers.

■ You can also adjust
blending modes with the
drop-down list in the Layers
palette. In this example, the
blend mode has been
changed to Multiply.

...GLOW

...APPLYING DROP SHADOW...

EDIT LAYER EFFECT

LOCKING
OUTER
GLOW

ANGLE

LOCK

DISTANC

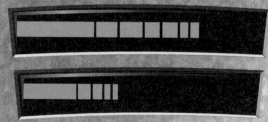

EMBOSS

MULTIPLE EFFECTS

LOGOTEXT

CHAPTER 10

Applying Layer Effects

You can apply special effects to layers by applying Photoshop's built-in layer effects. The effects let you add shadows, glows, and 3D appearances to your layers. Photoshop's Styles palette lets you easily apply predefined combinations of effects to your image.

SPREAD   SIZE

DEPTH   ALTITUDE

NOISE   VALUES   PREVIEW

APPLY A DROP SHADOW

You can apply a drop shadow to make a layer look like it is raised off the image canvas.

APPLY A DROP SHADOW

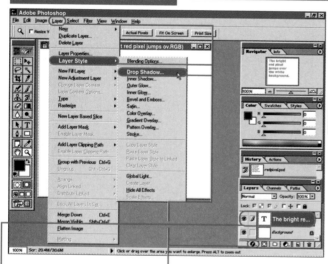

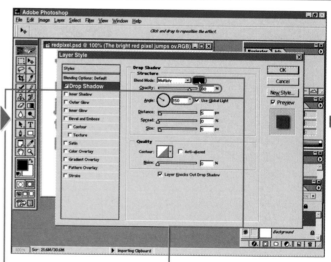

1 Select the layer to which you want to add a drop shadow.

■ If the Layers palette is not visible, you can click **Window** and **Show Layers** to display it.

2 Click **Layer**.

3 Click **Layer Style**.

4 Click **Drop Shadow**.

■ You can also click the Layer Effects button (⊘) and select **Drop Shadow**.

Note: Perform Steps 5 through 10 if you want to enter your own settings. If you want to use the default settings, you can skip to Step 11.

5 Type an Opacity value to specify the shadow's darkness.

6 Click the color swatch to select a shadow color.

Note: The default shadow color is black.

7 Type an Angle value to specify in which direction the shadow is displaced.

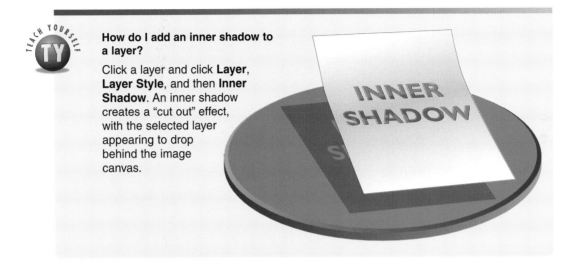

How do I add an inner shadow to a layer?

Click a layer and click **Layer**, **Layer Style**, and then **Inner Shadow**. An inner shadow creates a "cut out" effect, with the selected layer appearing to drop behind the image canvas.

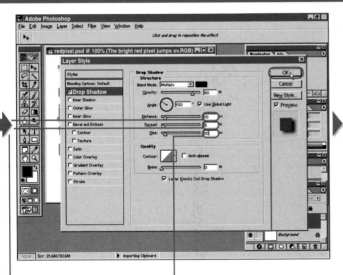

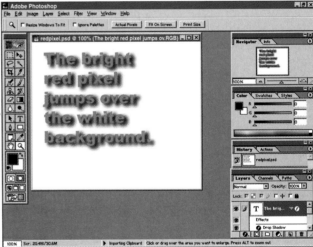

8 Type a distance to specify how far the shadow is displaced.

9 Type a Spread value to specify the fuzziness of the shadow's edge.

10 Type a Size value to specify the size of the shadow's edge.

11 Click **OK**.

■ Photoshop creates a shadow in back of the selected layer.

Note: In this example, the effect was applied to a layer of type. For more information about type, see Chapter 12.

APPLY AN OUTER GLOW

The outer glow effect adds faint coloring to the outside edge of a layer.

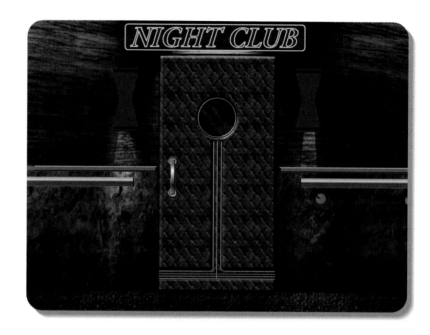

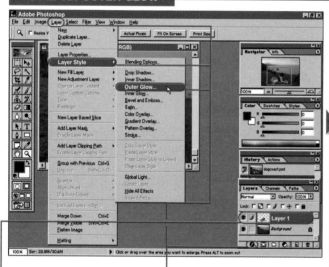

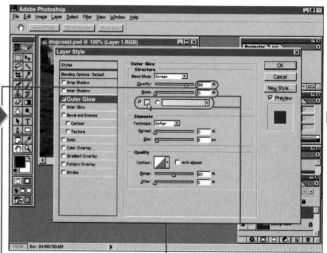

1 Select the layer to which you want to add an outer glow.

■ If the Layers palette is not visible, you can click **Window** and **Show Layers** to display it.

2 Click **Layer**.

3 Click **Layer Style**.

4 Click **Outer Glow**.

■ You can also click [icon] and select **Outer Glow**.

Note: Perform Steps 5 through 9 if you want to enter your own Outer Glow settings. If you want to use the default settings, you can skip to Step 10.

5 Type an Opacity value to specify the glow's darkness.

6 Specify a Noise value to add speckling to the glow.

7 Click the color swatch to choose the color of the glow. (Or you can choose from a series of preset color combinations from the drop-down list.)

TEACH YOURSELF
TY

How do I give elements in a layer an inner glow?

Click a layer and click **Layer**, **Layer Style**, and then **Inner Glow**. An inner glow adds color to the inside edge of a layer.

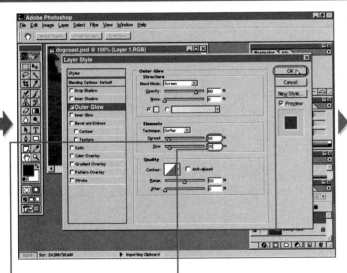

8 Type a Spread value to determine the fuzziness of the glow.

9 Type a Size value to specify the size of the glow.

10 Click **OK**.

■ Photoshop creates a glow around the outer edge of the selected layer.

APPLY BEVELING AND EMBOSSING

You can bevel and emboss a layer to give it a three-dimensional look.

APPLY BEVELING AND EMBOSSING

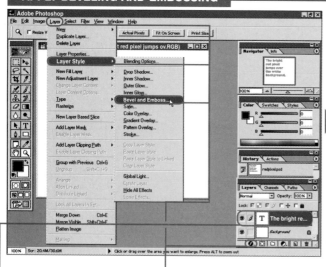

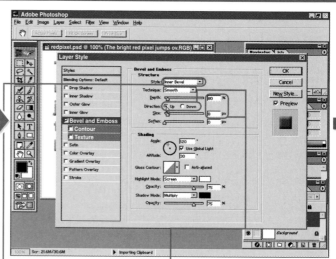

1 Select the layer that you want to bevel and emboss.

■ If the Layers palette is not visible, you can click **Window** and **Show Layers** to display it.

2 Click **Layer**.

3 Click **Layer Style**.

4 Click **Bevel and Emboss**.

■ You can also click 🔳 and select **Bevel and Emboss**.

Note: Perform Steps 5 Through 9 if you want to enter your own settings. If you want to use the default settings, you can skip to Step 10.

5 Select an effect style. **Inner Bevel** creates a three-dimensional look.

6 Specify the direction of the effect's shadowing (○ changes to ⊙).

7 Type Depth and Size values to control the magnitude of the effect.

When would I use the Bevel and Emboss effect?

The effect can be useful for creating three-dimensional buttons for Web pages or multimedia applications. For example, to create such a 3D button, you can apply Bevel and Emboss to a colored rectangle and then lay type over it.

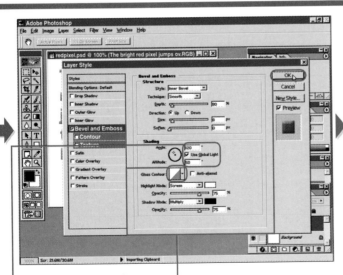

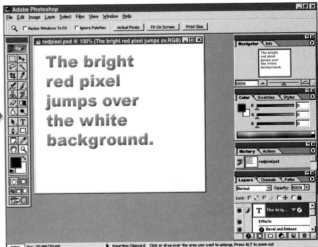

8 Specify the direction of the shading with the Angle and Altitude values.

9 Click ⊞ and select one of the Gloss Contour settings to apply abstract effects to your layer.

10 Click **OK**.

■ Photoshop applies the bevel and emboss settings to the layer.

Note: In this example, the effect was applied to a layer of type. For more about type, see Chapter 12.

APPLY MULTIPLE EFFECTS TO A LAYER

You can apply multiple
layer effects to layers in
your image. This enables
to you to style your
layers in complex ways.

APPLY MULTIPLE EFFECTS TO A LAYER

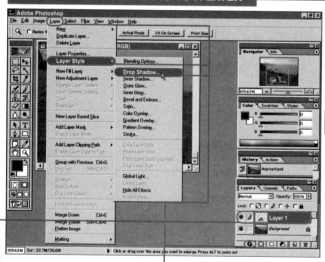

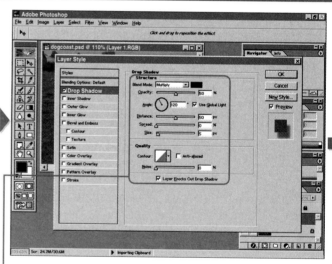

 Select the layer to which
you want to apply the effects.

■ If the Layers palette
is not visible, you can click
Window and **Show Layers**.

■ In this example, drop
shadow and color overlay
effects are applied.

APPLY THE FIRST EFFECT

-2 Click **Layer**.

-3 Click **Layer Style**.

-4 Click the name of the first
effect that you want to apply.

-5 Specify the configuration
values for the first effect.

**How do I turn off layer effects
that I have applied?**

When you apply an effect to a
layer, the effect gets added to
the Layers palette. (You may
have to click ▷ to see a layer's
effects [▷ changes to ▽].) You
can temporarily turn off an
effect by clicking 👁 in the
Layers palette. (You
can turn the effect on
by clicking the now-
empty box again to
make 👁 reappear.)

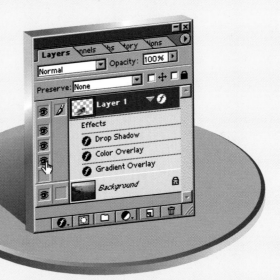

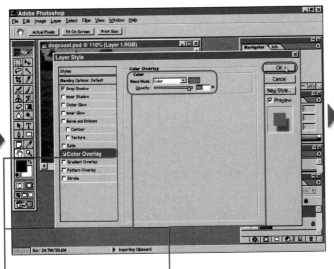

APPLY THE SECOND EFFECT

6 Click the next effect (☐
changes to ☑).

7 Specify the configuration
values for this effect.

■ In this example, a green
overlay is applied to the layer.

■ You can apply other effects
to the layer by repeating
Steps **6** and **7**.

8 Click **OK**.

■ Photoshop applies the
effects to the layer.

EDIT A LAYER EFFECT

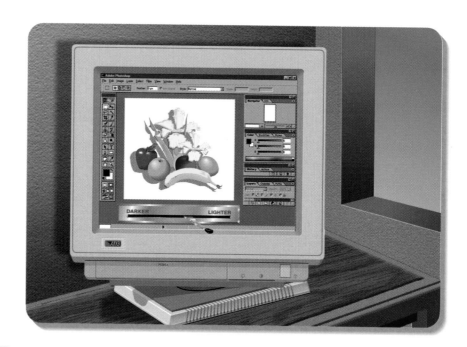

You can edit a layer effect that you have applied to your image. This lets you fine-tune the effect to achieve an appearance that suits you.

EDIT A LAYER EFFECT

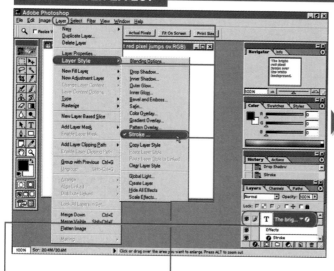

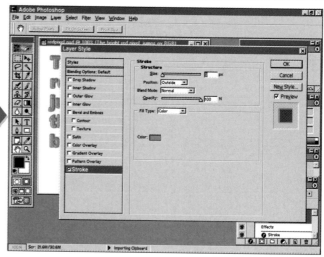

1 Select the layer whose effect you want to edit.

■ If the Layers palette is not visible, you can click **Window** and **Show Layers**.

■ This example shows editing the color stroked around text.

2 Click **Layer**.

3 Click **Layer Style**.

4 Click **Stroke**.

■ You can also double-click the effect in the Layers palette.

■ Photoshop displays the current configuration values for the effect.

188

**How do I keep a layer effect from
accidentally being changed?**

You can lock a layer and its effects by
selecting the layer and checking the ▣
check box in the Layers palette (❑ changes
to 3). The layer is then locked, which means
that you cannot change its styles or apply
any more Photoshop commands to it. (To
keep a layer from moving — while still
allowing all other commands — select
the layer and check the ⊞ check box
in the Layers palette.)

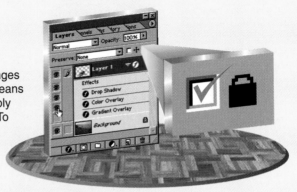

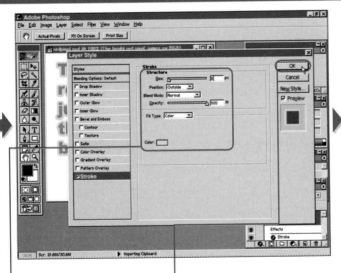

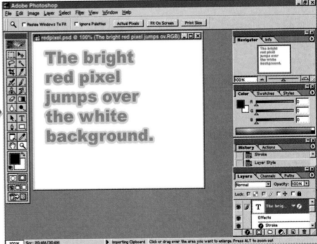

5 Edit the values in the
Layer Style dialog box.

■ This example shows
broadening and recoloring
of the stroke effect.

6 Click **OK**.

■ Photoshop applies the
edited effect to the layer.

■ You can edit an effect as
many times as you want.

*Note: In this example, the effect was
applied to a layer of type. For more
about type, see Chapter 12.*

APPLY STYLES

You can apply a Photoshop style to a layer to give the layer a colorful or textured look. Styles are predefined combinations of Photoshop effects (such as Drop Shadow and Outer Glow).

APPLY A STYLE

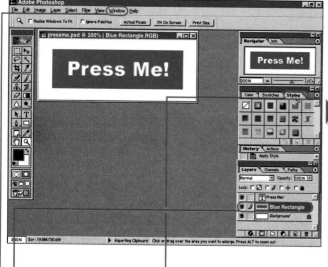

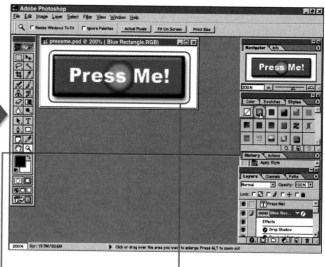

1 Select the layer to which you want to apply a style.

■ If the Layers palette is not visible, you can click **Window** and **Show Layers** to display it.

2 Click the Styles palette tab to display Photoshop's styles.

3 Click a style.

■ Photoshop applies the style to the selected layer.

How do I create my own custom styles?

To create a custom style, first apply one or more effects (such as Drop Shadow, Outer Glow, and others) to a layer in your image. With the layer selected in the Layers palette, click the Styles ⊙ and click **New Style**. A dialog box appears that lets you name your custom style. Click **OK** in the dialog box to add an icon for your new style to the Styles palette.

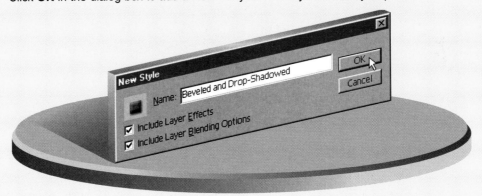

ACCESS MORE STYLES

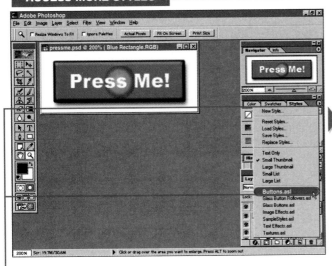

1 Click the Styles ⊙.

2 Click a set of styles.

■ Photoshop displays a dialog box that lets you replace the current styles with the new set or append the new set.

3 Click **OK** or **Append**.

■ The new styles are added to the Styles palette.

■ In this example, the new styles have been appended to the current ones.

CHAPTER 11

Applying Filters

With Photoshop's filters, you can quickly and easily apply enhancements to your image, including artistic effects, texture effects, and distortions. Filters can help you correct defects in your images or let you turn a photograph into something resembling an impressionist painting.

Artistic filters make your image look as though it was created with traditional artisitic techniques. The Dry Brush filter, one example of an Artistic filter, applies a painted effect by converting similarly colored areas in your image to solid colors.

APPLY AN ARTISTIC FILTER: THE DRY BRUSH FILTER

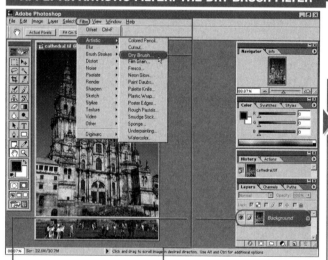

1 Select the layer to which you want to apply the filter.

Note: In this example, the image has a single background layer.

■ If you want to apply the filter to just part of your image, make the selection with a selection tool.

2 Click **Filter**.

3 Click **Artistic**.

4 Click **Dry Brush**.

■ A small window displays a preview of the filter's effect.

5 Click the – or + button to zoom out or in.

6 Fine-tune the filter effect by adjusting the Brush Size, Brush Detail, and Texture values.

What does the Sponge filter do?

The Sponge filter reduces detail and modifies the shapes in an image to create the effect you get when applying a damp sponge to a wet painting. Apply it by clicking **Filter**, **Artistic**, and then **Sponge**.

■ In this example, the dry-brush effect has been thickened by increasing Brush Size and decreasing Brush Detail.

7 Click **OK**.

■ Photoshop applies the filter.

APPLY A BLUR FILTER: THE GAUSSIAN BLUR FILTER

Photoshop's Blur filters reduce the amount of detail in your image. The Gaussian Blur filter has advantages over the other Blur filters in that you can control the amount of blur added.

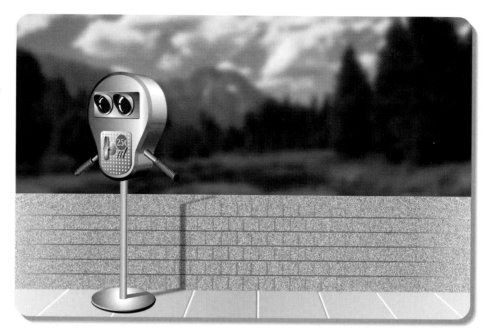

APPLY A BLUR FILTER: THE GAUSSIAN BLUR FILTER

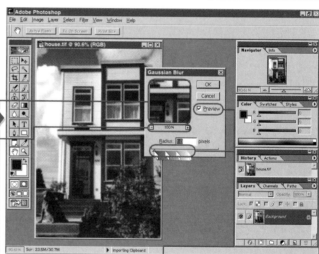

1 Select the layer to which you want to apply the filter.

Note: In this example, the image has a single background layer.

■ If you want to apply the filter to just part of your image, make the selection with a selection tool.

2 Click **Filter**.

3 Click **Blur**.

4 Click **Gaussian Blur**.

■ A small window displays a preview of the filter's effect.

5 Click the – or + button to zoom out or in.

6 Click **Preview** to preview the effect in the main window (☐ changes to ☑).

7 Click and drag the Radius slider to control the amount of blur added.

How do I add directional blurring to an image?

You can add directional blur to your image with the Motion Blur filter. This can add a sense of motion to your image. Apply it by selecting **Filter**, **Blur**, and then **Motion Blur**.

■ In this example, the amount of blur has been increased by boosting the Radius value.

8 Click **OK**.

■ Photoshop applies the filter.

APPLY A BRUSH STROKES FILTER:
THE CROSSHATCH FILTER

Photoshop's Brush Strokes filters make your image look painted. For example, the Crosshatch filter adds diagonal, overlapping brush-stroke effects to your image. Similar to the Dry Brush filter (see the section "Apply an Artistic Filter: The Dry Brush Filter"), the Crosshatch filter converts similarly colored areas in your image to solid colors to produce its effect.

APPLY A BRUSH STROKES FILTER: THE CROSSHATCH FILTER

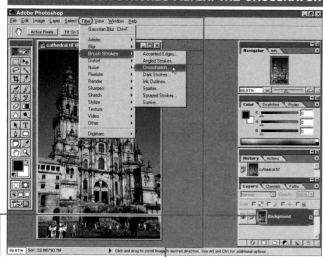

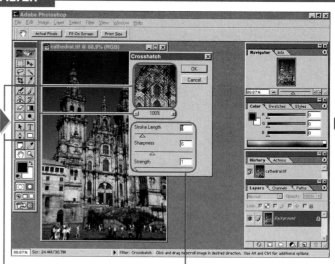

1 Select the layer to which you want to apply the filter.

Note: In this example, the image has a single background layer.

■ If you want to apply the filter to just part of your image, make the selection with a selection tool.

2 Click **Filter**.

3 Click **Brush Strokes**.

4 Click **Crosshatch**.

■ A small window displays a preview of the filter's effect.

5 Click the – or + button to zoom out or in.

6 Fine-tune the filter effect by adjusting the Stroke Length, Sharpness, and Strength values.

What does the Ink Outlines filter do?

The Ink Outlines filter produces an eery, high-contrast effect in your image by outlining edges with black streaks. Apply it by clicking **Filter**, **Brush Strokes**, and then **Ink Outlines**.

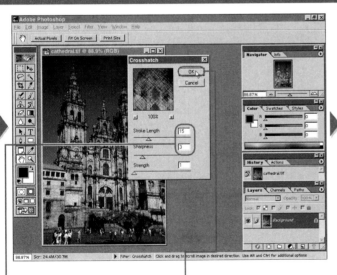

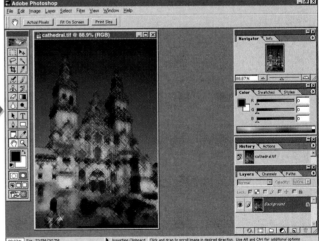

■ In this example, the brush-stroke effect has been intensified by increasing the Stroke Length value and decreasing the Sharpness value.

7 Click **OK**.

■ Photoshop applies the filter.

APPLY A DISTORT FILTER: THE SPHERIZE FILTER

Photoshop's Distort filters stretch and squeeze areas of your image. For example, the Spherize filter produces a fun-house effect. It makes your image look like it is being reflected off a mirrored sphere.

APPLY A DISTORT FILTER: THE SPHERIZE FILTER

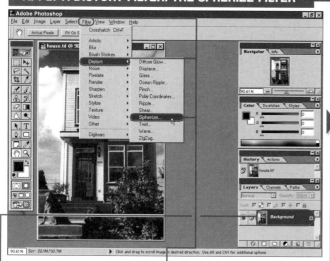

1 Select the layer to which you want to apply the filter.

Note: In this example, the image has a single background layer.

■ If you want to apply the filter to just part of your image, make the selection with a selection tool.

2 Click **Filter**.

3 Click **Distort**.

4 Click **Spherize**.

■ A small window displays a preview of the filter's effect.

5 Click the – or + button to zoom out or in.

6 Click and drag the Amount slider to control the amount of distortion added.

What happens when I type a negative value in the Amount field of the Spherize dialog box?

A negative value "squeezes" the shapes in your image instead of expanding them. The Pinch filter (also under the **Filter** and **Distort** menu selections) produces a similar effect.

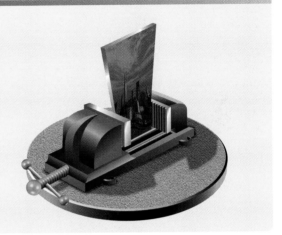

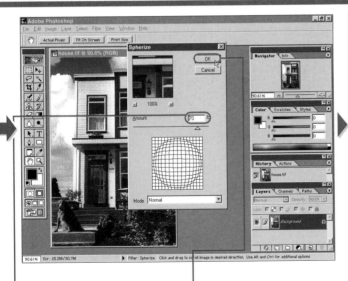

■ In this example, the intensity of the spherize effect has been decreased.

7 Click **OK**.

■ Photoshop applies the filter.

APPLY A NOISE FILTER: THE ADD NOISE FILTER

Filters in the Noise menu add or remove graininess in your image. You can add graininess with the Add Noise filter.

APPLY A NOISE FILTER: THE ADD NOISE FILTER

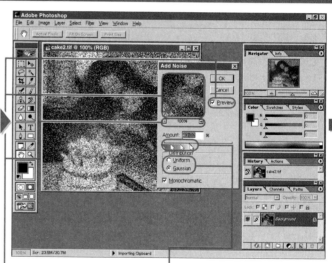

1 Select the layer to which you want to apply the filter.

Note: In this example, the image has a single background layer.

■ If you want to apply the filter to just part of your image, make the selection with a selection tool.

2 Click **Filter**.

3 Click **Noise**.

4 Click **Add Noise**.

■ A small window displays a preview.

5 Click – or + to zoom.

6 Click **Preview** to preview the effect in the main window (☐ changes to ☑).

7 Click and drag the Amount slider to control the amount of noise added.

8 Select the way you want the noise distributed (○ changes to ◉).

Note: Uniform spreads the noise more evenly than Gaussian.

What does the Monochromatic setting in the Add Noise dialog box do?

If you select Monochromatic, noise will be added by lightening or darkening pixels in your image. Pixel hues will stay the same. At high settings with the Monochromatic setting on, the filter produces a television-static effect.

■ In this example, the Amount value has been decreased.

9 Click **OK**.

■ Photoshop applies the filter.

APPLY A PIXELATE FILTER: THE POINTILLIZE FILTER

The Pixelate filters divide areas of your image into solid-colored shapes. The Pointillize filter, one example of a Pixelate filter, re-creates your image using colored dots.

Pointillism is a painting technique that was popularized by impressionist artists of the nineteenth century.

APPLY A PIXELATE FILTER: THE POINTILLIZE FILTER

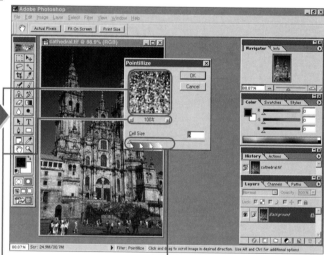

1 Select the layer to which you want to apply the filter.

Note: In this example, the image has a single background layer.

■ If you want to apply the filter to just part of your image, make the selection with a selection tool.

2 Click **Filter**.

3 Click **Pixelate**.

4 Click **Pointillize**.

■ A small window displays a preview of the filter's effect.

5 Click the − or + button to zoom out or in.

6 Click and drag the Cell Size slider to adjust the size of the dots.

Note: The size can range from 3 to 300.

What does the Mosaic filter do?

The Mosaic filter converts your image to a set of solid-color squares. You can control the size of the squares in the filter's dialog box. Apply it by clicking **Filter**, **Pixelate**, and then **Mosaic**.

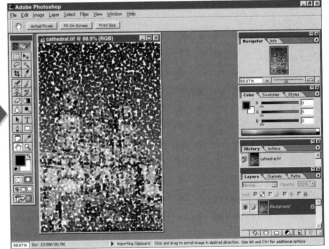

■ In this example, the Cell Size has been slightly increased.

7 Click **OK**.

■ Photoshop applies the filter.

APPLY A RENDER FILTER: THE LIGHTING EFFECTS FILTER

The Render filters use numeric techniques to apply effects to your image. The Lighting Effects filter, for example, lets you add spotlight and other lighting ehancements.

APPLY A RENDER FILTER: THE LIGHTING EFFECTS FILTER

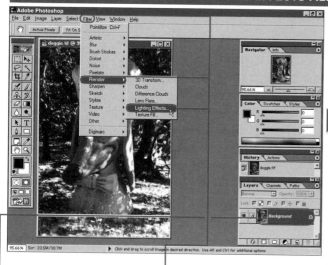

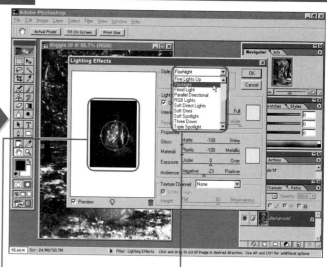

■ Select the layer to which you want to apply the filter.

Note: In this example, the image has a single background layer.

■ If you want to apply the filter to just part of your image, make the selection with a selection tool.

■2 Click **Filter**.

■3 Click **Render**.

■4 Click **Lighting Effects**.

■ Photoshop displays a small preview of the effect.

■5 Click ▼ and choose a lighting style.

What is a lens flare, and how can I add it to an image?

Lens flare is the extra flash of light that sometimes appears in a photo when too much light enters a camera lens. Photographers try to avoid this effect, but if you want to add it, you can use the Lens Flare filter. (The effect can make your digital image look more like an old-fashioned photograph.) Apply it by clicking **Filter**, **Render**, and then **Lens Flare**.

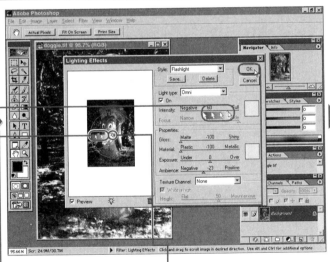

6 Click and drag the slider to control the light intensity.

7 Adjust the position and shape of the lighting by clicking and dragging the handles in the preview window.

■ You can click and drag the center point to change where the light is centered.

8 Click **OK**.

■ Photoshop applies the filter.

APPLY A SHARPEN FILTER: THE UNSHARP MASK FILTER

Photoshop's Sharpen filters intensify the detail and reduce blurring in your image. The Unsharp Mask filter has advantages over the other Sharpen filters in that it lets you control the amount of sharpening applied.

APPLY A SHARPEN FILTER: THE UNSHARP MASK FILTER

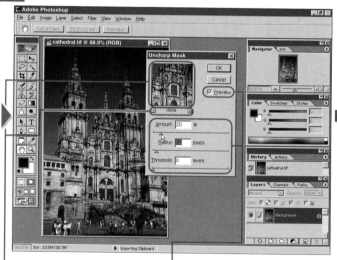

1 Select the layer to which you want to apply the filter.

Note: In this example, the image has a single background layer.

■ If you want to apply the filter to just part of your image, make the selection with a selection tool.

2 Click **Filter**.

3 Click **Sharpen**.

4 Click **Unsharp Mask**.

■ A small window displays a preview of the filter's effect.

5 Click the – or + button to zoom out or in.

6 Click **Preview** to preview the effect in the main window (☐ changes to ☑).

7 Click and drag the sliders to control the amount of sharpening applied to the image.

When should sharpening be applied?

It is a good idea to sharpen an image after you have changed its size because changing an image's size will add blurring. Applying the Unsharp Mask filter can also help clarify scanned images.

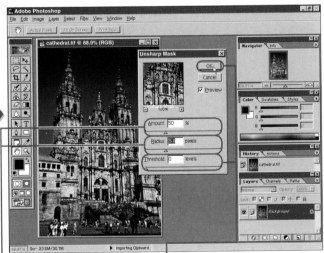

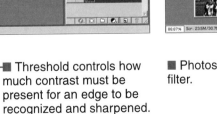

■ Amount controls the overall amount of sharpening.

■ Radius controls whether sharpening is confined to edges in the image (low Radius setting) or added across the entire image (high Radius setting).

■ Threshold controls how much contrast must be present for an edge to be recognized and sharpened.

8 Click **OK**.

■ Photoshop applies the filter.

APPLY A SKETCH FILTER: THE CHARCOAL FILTER

The Sketch filters add outlining effects to your image. The Charcoal filter, for example, makes an image look as if it was sketched by using charcoal on paper.

APPLY A SKETCH FILTER: THE CHARCOAL FILTER

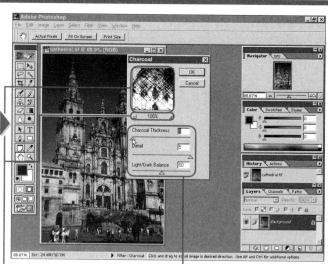

1 Select the layer to which you want to apply the filter.

■ If you want to apply the filter to just part of your image, make the selection with a selection tool.

■ The foreground is used as the charcoal color and the background as the paper color.

2 Click **Filter**.

3 Click **Sketch**.

4 Click **Charcoal**.

■ A small window displays a preview of the filter's effect.

5 Click the − or + button to zoom out or in.

6 Click and drag the sliders to control the filter's effect.

What does the Photocopy filter do?

The Photocopy filter converts shadows and midtones in your image to the foreground color and highlights in your image to the background color. The result is an image that looks photocopied. You can apply the Photocopy filter by clicking **Filter**, **Sketch**, and then **Photocopy**.

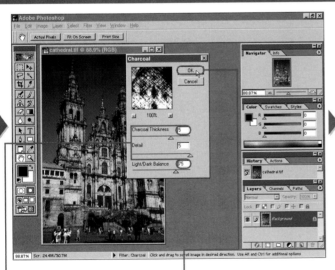

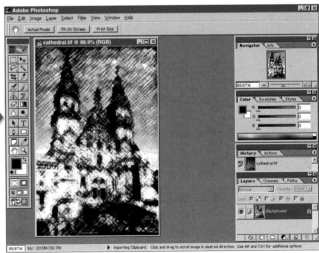

■ In this example, the thickness of the charcoal strokes has been increased. The Light/Dark Balance setting has also been increased to darken the image.

7 Click **OK**.

■ Photoshop applies the filter.

APPLY A STYLIZE FILTER: THE GLOWING EDGES FILTER

The Glowing Edges filter, one example of a Stylize filter, applies a neon effect to the edges in your image. Areas between the edges are turned black. Other Stylize filters produce similarly extreme artistic effects.

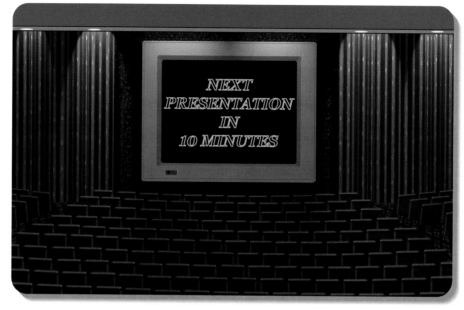

APPLY A STYLIZE FILTER: THE GLOWING EDGES FILTER

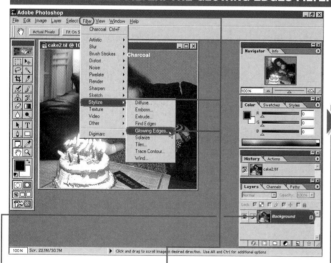

■1 Select the layer to which you want to apply the filter.

Note: In this example, the image has a single background layer.

■ If you want to apply the filter to just part of your image, make the selection with a selection tool.

■2 Click **Filter**.

■3 Click **Stylize**.

■4 Click **Glowing Edges**.

■ A small window displays a preview of the filter's effect.

■5 Click the – or + button to zoom out or in.

■6 Click and drag the sliders to control intensity of the glow added to the edges in the image.

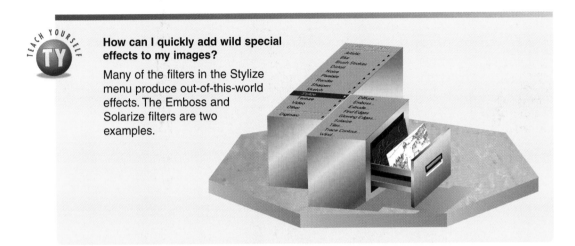

How can I quickly add wild special effects to my images?

Many of the filters in the Stylize menu produce out-of-this-world effects. The Emboss and Solarize filters are two examples.

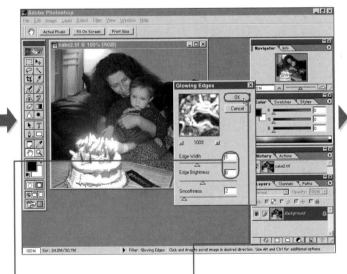

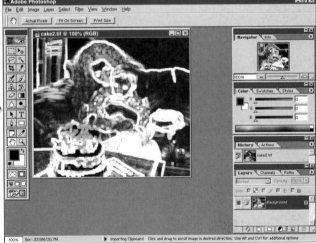

■ In this example, the Edge Width and Edge Brightness values have been increased to intensify the neon effect.

7 Click **OK**.

■ Photoshop applies the filter.

You can overlay different textures on your image with the Texturizer filter. The other Texture filters let you apply other patterns.

APPLY A TEXTURE FILTER: THE TEXTURIZER FILTER

1 Select the layer to which you want to apply the filter.

Note: In this example, the image has a single background layer.

■ If you want to apply the filter to just part of your image, make the selection with a selection tool.

2 Click **Filter**.

3 Click **Texture**.

4 Click **Texturizer**.

■ A small window displays a preview of the filter's effect.

5 Click the – or + button to zoom out or in.

6 Click 🔽 and select a texture to apply.

What does the Stained Glass filter do?

The Stained Glass filter converts small areas of your image to different solid-color shapes, similar to those you might see in a stained-glass window. A foreground-color border separates the shapes. Apply it by selecting **Filter**, **Texture**, and then **Stained Glass**.

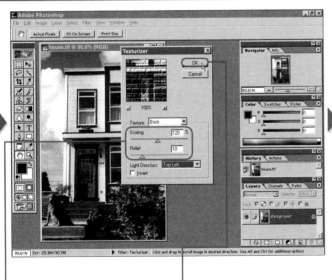

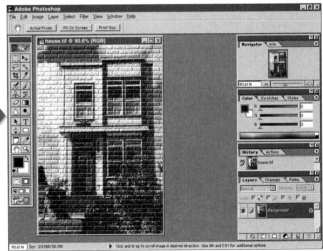

7 Adjust the sliders to control the intensity of the overlaid texture.

8 Click **OK**.

■ Photoshop applies the filter.

APPLY A FILTER FROM THE OTHER SUBMENU: THE OFFSET FILTER

The filters in the Other submenu produce interesting effects that do not fall under the other menu descriptions. For example, you can shift your image horizontally or vertically in the image window using the Other menu's Offset filter.

APPLY A FILTER FROM THE OTHER SUBMENU: THE OFFSET FILTER

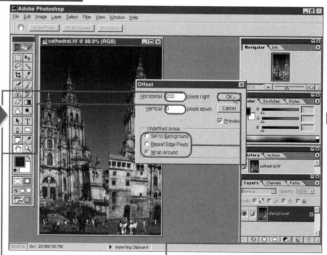

1 Select the layer to which you want to apply the filter.

Note: In this example, the image has a single background layer.

■ If you want to apply the filter to just a select part of your image, make the selection with a selection tool.

2 Click **Filter**.

3 Click **Other**.

4 Click **Offset**.

5 Type a horizontal offset.

6 Type a vertical offset.

7 Select how you want pixels at the edge to be treated (○ changes to ⦿).

8 Click **OK**.

How do I make a seamless tile?

Seamless tiles are images that when laid side by side leave no noticeable seam where they meet. They are often used as background images for Web pages. To create a seamless tile, start with an evenly textured image; then offset the image horizontally and vertically; then clean up the resulting seams with the Rubber Stamp tool (📥) (see Chapter 7 for information on using the Rubber Stamp tool). The resulting image will tile seamlessly.

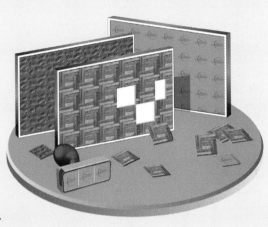

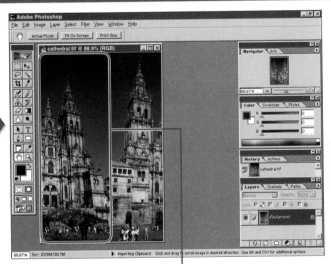

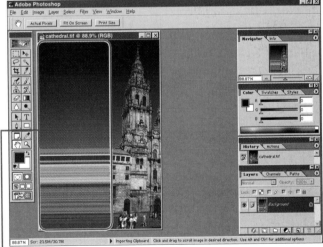

■ In this example, the image has been shifted horizontally (to the right) by adding a positive value to the horizontal field.

■ Wrap Around was selected, so the pixels that leave the right edge of the image reappear on the left edge.

■ In this example, the same offset was applied but with the Repeat Edge Pixels selected. This creates a streaked effect at the left edge.

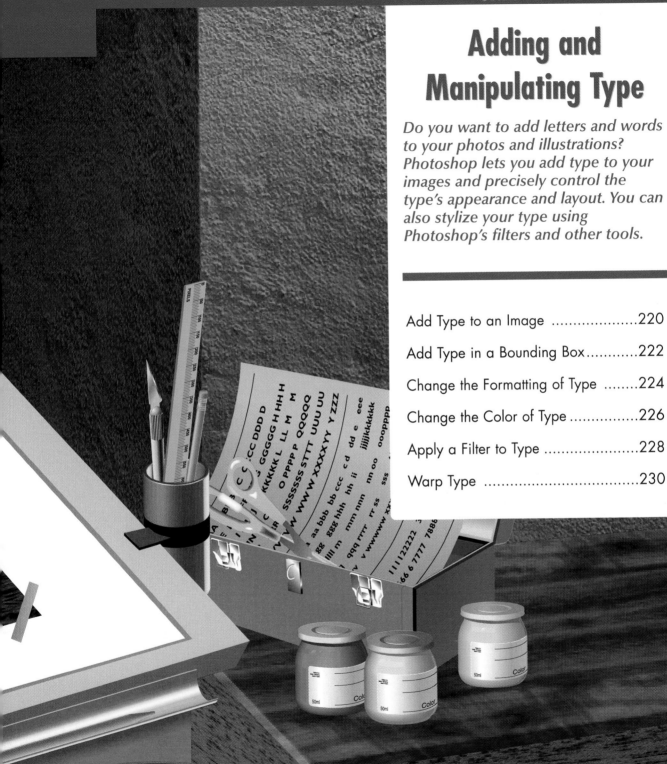

CHAPTER 12

Adding and Manipulating Type

Do you want to add letters and words to your photos and illustrations? Photoshop lets you add type to your images and precisely control the type's appearance and layout. You can also stylize your type using Photoshop's filters and other tools.

ADD TYPE TO AN IMAGE

Adding type enables you to label elements in your image or use letters and words in artistic ways.

ADD TYPE TO AN IMAGE

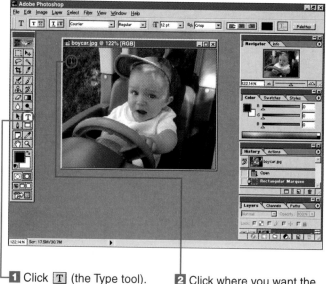

1 Click **T** (the Type tool).

2 Click where you want the new type to appear.

3 Click ▼ and select a font, style, and size for your type.

4 Click the color swatch to select a color for your type.

Note: The foreground color is applied by default.

How do I reposition my type?

Added type is placed in its own layer. You can move the layer with the Move tool ⊕. Select the layer of type, click ⊕, and click and drag to reposition your type.

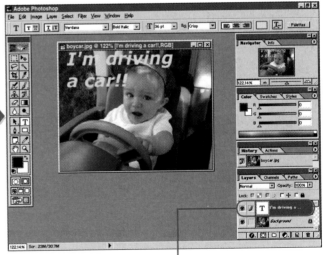

5 Type your text. To create a line break, press Enter (Return).

6 When you finish typing your text, press Enter on your keyboard's number pad or click a different tool in the toolbox.

■ The type is placed in its own layer.

You can add type inside a *bounding box* to constrain where the type appears and how it wraps.

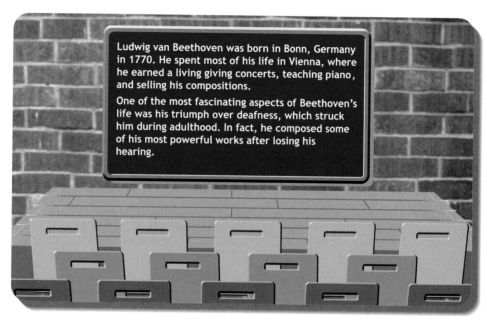

Ludwig van Beethoven was born in Bonn, Germany in 1770. He spent most of his life in Vienna, where he earned a living giving concerts, teaching piano, and selling his compositions.

One of the most fascinating aspects of Beethoven's life was his triumph over deafness, which struck him during adulthood. In fact, he composed some of his most powerful works after losing his hearing.

ADD TYPE IN A BOUNDING BOX

1 Click ⊤.

2 Click and drag inside the image to define the bounding box.

3 Click and drag the handles of the bounding box to adjust its dimensions.

4 Click and drag the center point of the bounding box to move the box.

5 Select the formatting of the type to be added.

How do I format paragraph text inside a bounding box?

With ⊤ selected, click the text inside the box to highlight it. Then click **Window** and **Show Paragraph** to display the Paragraph palette. The palette enables you to control the alignment, indenting, and hyphenation of the text inside a bounding box. (A limited selection of the palette's commands can also be performed on text that is not constrained by a bounding box.)

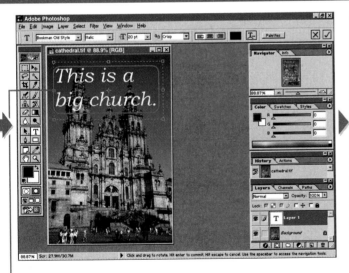

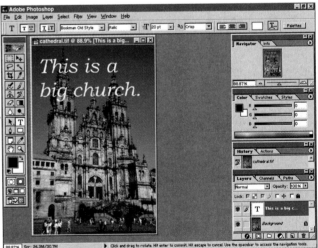

6 Type your text.

■ Your text appears inside the bounding box.

Note: When a line of text hits the edge of the bounding box, it automatically wraps to the next line.

7 When you finish typing your text, press `Enter` on your keyboard's number pad or click a different tool in the toolbox.

■ The bounding box disappears.

■ To make the box reappear (in order to change its dimensions), click ⊤ and click the text.

CHANGE THE FORMATTING OF TYPE

You can change the font, style, size, and other characteristics of your type.

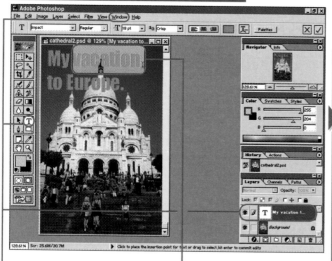

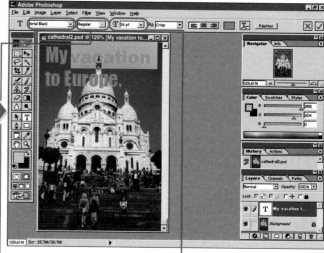

■1 Click **T**.

■2 Select the type layer that you would like to edit.

■ If the Layers palette is not visible, you can click **Window** and then **Show Layers** to view it.

■3 Click and drag to select some text.

Note: You can press Ctrl + A *(⌘ + A) to select all the text in a layer.*

■4 Click ▼ and select a font.

■5 Click ▼ and select the type's style.

■6 Click ▼ and select the type's size.

How do I rotate type?

You can rotate type in your image by rotating the layer that contains the type. Choose the layer in the Layers palette and click **Edit** and **Free Transform**. A bounding box appears. You can click and drag outside the box to rotate the layer. Press **Enter** (**Return**) to apply the rotation.

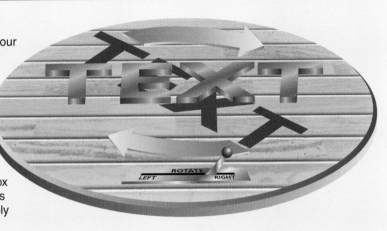

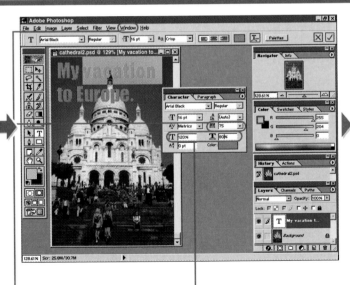

7 To display more commands, click **Window** and then **Show Character**.

8 Adjust the spacing between characters by specifying a value (positive or negative) in the Tracking box.

9 Stretch the characters horizontally or vertically by typing percentage values in the scale fields.

10 Press Enter on your keyboard's number pad or click another tool to deselect the type.

■ Photoshop applies the formatting to your type.

CHANGE THE COLOR OF TYPE

You can change the color of your type to make it blend or contrast with the rest of the image.

CHANGE THE COLOR OF TYPE

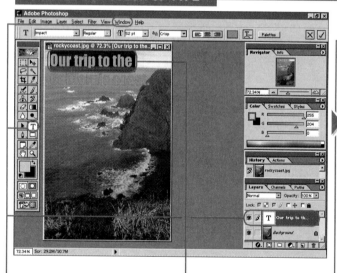

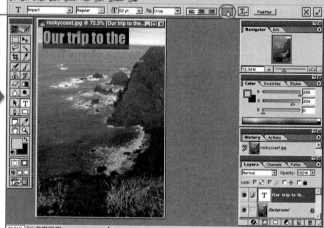

■1 Click T.

■2 Click the type layer that you would like to edit.

■ If the Layers palette is not visible, you can click **Window** and then **Show Layers** to view it.

■3 Click and drag to select some text.

Note: You can press Ctrl + A *(*⌘+A*) to select all the text in a layer.*

■4 Click the Color swatch.

What is antialiasing?

Antialiasing is the process of adding semitransparent pixels to curved edges in digital images to make the edges appear more smooth. You can apply antialiasing to type in Photoshop to improve its appearance. (Text that is not antialiased often looks jagged.) You can control the presence and style of your type's antialiasing with the Options bar.

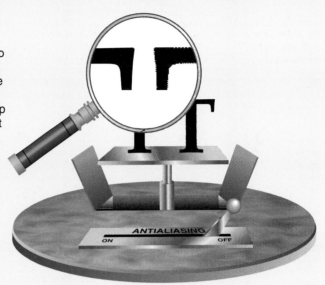

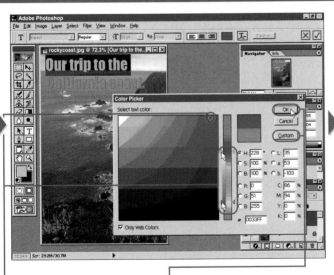

■ The Color Picker dialog box appears.

5 Click a color.

■ You can click and drag the slider to change the colors that are displayed in the window.

■ You can also click **Custom** to choose from different color palettes.

6 Click **OK**.

7 Press Enter on your keyboard's number pad or click another tool to deselect the text.

■ Photoshop changes the text to the new color.

APPLY A FILTER TO TYPE

To apply a filter to type, you must first rasterize it. Rasterizing converts your type layer into a regular Photoshop layer. Rasterized type can no longer be edited using the type tools.

APPLY A FILTER TO TYPE

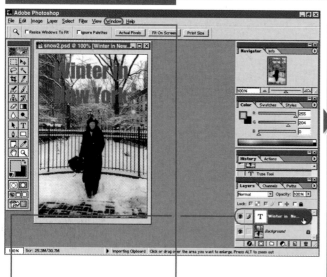

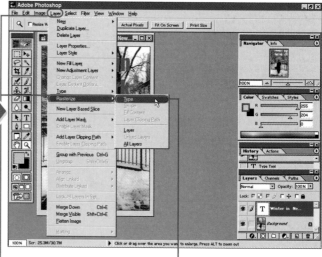

1 Select the type layer to which you would like to apply a filter.

■ If the Layers palette is not visible, you can click **Window** and then **Show Layers** to view it.

2 Click **Layer**.

3 Click **Rasterize**.

4 Click **Type**.

How can I create semitransparent type?

Select the type layer in the Layers palette and then reduce the layer's opacity to less than 100%. This will make the type semitransparent.

■ Photoshop converts the type layer to a regular layer.

■ Now you can apply a filter to the text.

■ In this example, noise was added to the type by clicking **Filter**, **Noise**, and then **Add Noise**.

Note: You can find more information about applying filters in Chapter 11.

WARP TYPE

Photoshop's Warp feature lets you easily bend and distort layers of type.

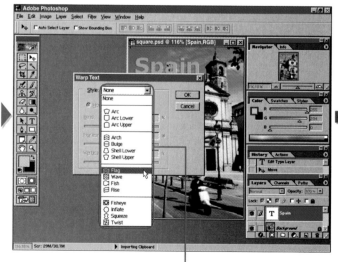

■1 Select the type layer that you would like to warp.

■ If the Layers palette is not visible, you can click **Window** and then **Show Layers** to view it.

■2 Click **Layer**.

■3 Click **Type**.

■4 Click **Warp Text**.

■ The Warp Text dialog box appears.

■5 Click the Style ▼ and select a warp style.

How do I insert an image into the outline of type?

First, select the image content that you would like to insert into your text and click **Edit** and **Copy**. (You can copy content from the same window or from another Photoshop window.) Convert your text layer to a regular layer by clicking **Layer**, **Rasterize**, and then **Type**. To insert the image into the type outline, Ctrl +click (option +click) the layer and then click **Edit** and **Paste Into**.

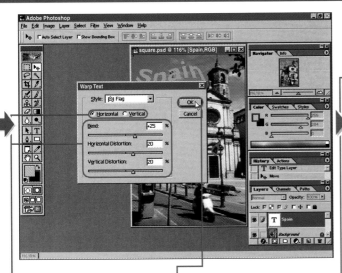

■6 Select an orientation for the warp effect (○ changes to ◉).

■7 Adjust the Bend and Distortion values.

Note: The Bend and Distortion values determine how the warp effect is applied. (At 0% for all values, no warp is applied.)

■8 Click **OK**.

■ Photoshop warps the text.

Note: You can still edit the style, color, and other characteristics of the type with warp applied.

CHAPTER 13

Automating Your Work

Sometimes you want to perform one or more commands on lots of images. Photoshop's actions let you automate repetitive imaging tasks by saving sequences of commands and applying them automatically to many image files. Other Photoshop commands let you streamline your work by automating the creation of Web photo galleries and buttons.

RECORD AN ACTION

You can record a sequence of commands as an action and replay them on other image files. This can save you time when you have a task in Photoshop that you need to repeat.

RECORD AN ACTION

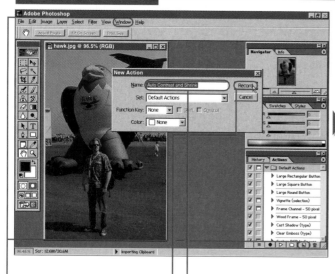

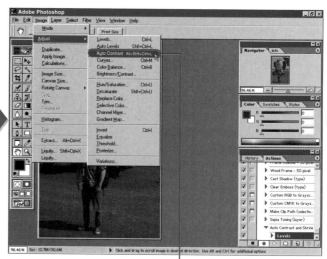

■1 Click **Window** and then **Show Actions** to open the Actions palette.

■2 Click the **New Action** button (🔲).

■3 Type in a name for your action.

■4 Click **Record**.

■5 Perform the sequence of commands that you would like to automate on the image.

■ In this example, the Auto Contrast command is first performed.

What if I make a mistake when recording my action?

You can try recording the action again by clicking **Record Again** in the Actions palette menu (click ⊙ in the upper-right corner). This will run through the same actions and let you apply different settings in the command dialog boxes. Alternatively, you can select the action, click 🗑 to delete the action, and try rerecording it.

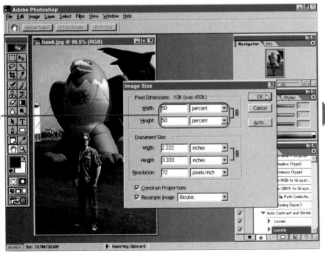

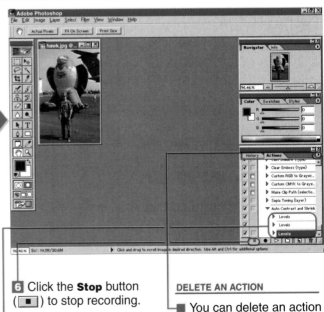

■ In this example, the image size is then reduced by 50% (by first clicking **Image** and **Image Size**).

6 Click the **Stop** button (■) to stop recording.

■ The Actions palette lists the commands performed under the name of the command.

DELETE AN ACTION

■ You can delete an action by clicking the **Delete** command from the Actions palette menu (click ⊙ in the palette's upper-right corner).

PLAY AN ACTION

You can play an action from the Actions palette on an image. This saves time by letting you execute multiple Photoshop commands with a single click.

PLAY A SINGLE ACTION

1 Click **Window** and then **Show Actions** to open the Actions palette.

2 Click to select the action that you would like to perform.

3 Click the **Play** button (▷) to perform the action on the image.

■ Photoshop applies the commands that make up the action to the image.

■ In this example, the action has rotated the image 25 degrees clockwise.

How do I assign a special key command to an action?

Double-click the action to open the Action Options dialog box. Select a key command by using the Function Key drop-down list. Then, to perform the action on an image, press the function key.

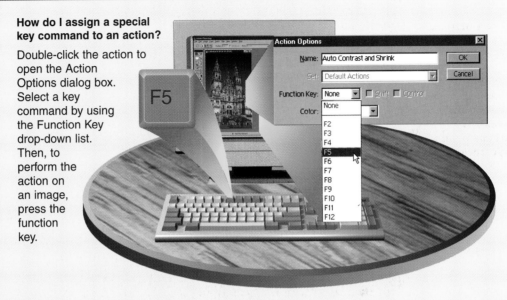

PLAY MULTIPLE ACTIONS

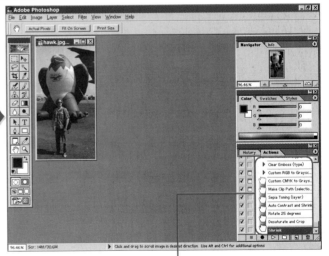

1 Click **Window** and then **Show Actions** to open the Actions palette.

2 Click to select the action that you would like to perform.

3 Shift +click to select other actions to perform.

Note: You can only perform multiple actions that are next to one another on the Actions palette.

4 Click ▷ to play the selected actions.

■ Photoshop performs the actions in the order they are listed in the Actions palette (top to bottom).

■ In this example, the image is desaturated and cropped and then has its size reduced.

■ To rearrange the order of actions in the Actions palette, you can click and drag them up and down.

Note: Not all actions can be played on all images. For example, you cannot play a Color Balance action on a grayscale image.

CREATE AND APPLY A DROPLET

You can store an action as an icon in a folder on your computer. You can then drag and drop image files or folders of image files onto this icon, called a *droplet,* to apply the action.

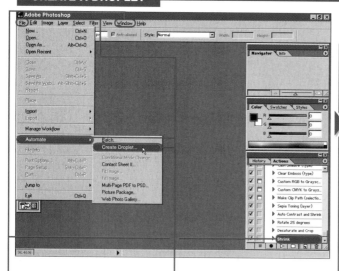

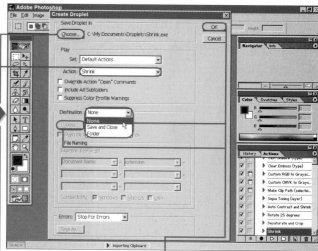

1 Click **Window** and then **Show Actions** to open the Actions palette.

2 Click the action that you would like to turn into a droplet.

3 Click **File**.

4 Click **Automate**.

5 Click **Create Droplet**.

■ The action you selected appears in the Action list.

■ If the action does not appear, click ☑ and select it.

6 Click **Choose** to select the folder in which to save the droplet.

7 Click ☑ and select a destination for the processed files.

■ If you select **Folder**, define the folder and choose how you would like the processed files to be saved.

8 Click **OK**.

238

How do I apply a droplet to multiple images?

Click and drag the folder containing the images onto the droplet. All the images inside the folder will be processed by Photoshop. (Non-image files in the folder will be ignored.)

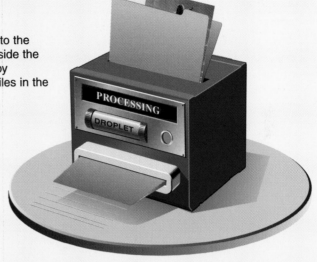

APPLY A DROPLET

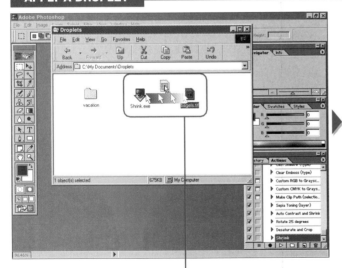

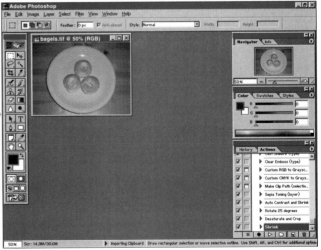

1 Navigate to the folder where you saved the droplet in the file directory system of your computer.

2 Click and drag an image file onto the droplet icon.

Note: You do not need to have Photoshop open to apply a droplet.

■ Photoshop applies the droplet's action to the image.

Note: There is no Undo command for droplet actions, so it may be a good idea to use copies of your original files when applying droplets.

CREATE A VIGNETTE EFFECT

You can create a soft edge around content in your image by using Photoshop's Vignette action.

Vignette is one of the actions that comes prebuilt in Photoshop's Actions palette. Other prebuilt actions let you perform useful tasks such as creating buttons (see "Create Buttons" in this chapter).

CREATE A VIGNETTE EFFECT

1 Select the Rectangular (▣) or Elliptical Marquee (◯) tool.

Note: To select the Elliptical Marquee tool, click and hold ▣ and select ◯ from the box that appears.

2 Click and drag inside the image to select the content you would like to surround with the vignette effect.

■ Photoshop will use the background color as the vignette background.

3 Click **Window** and then **Show Actions** to display the Actions palette.

4 Select the Vignette action.

5 Click ▷.

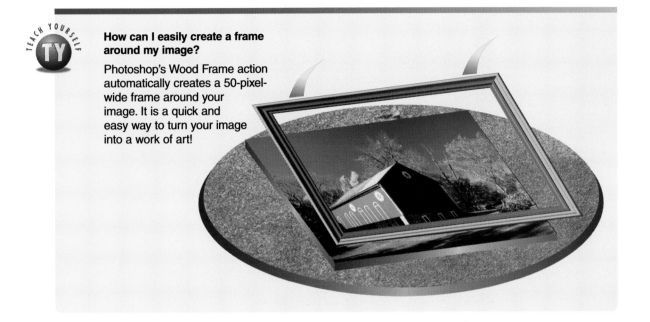

How can I easily create a frame around my image?

Photoshop's Wood Frame action automatically creates a 50-pixel-wide frame around your image. It is a quick and easy way to turn your image into a work of art!

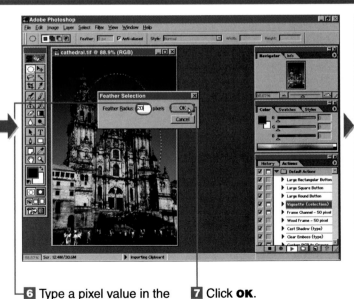

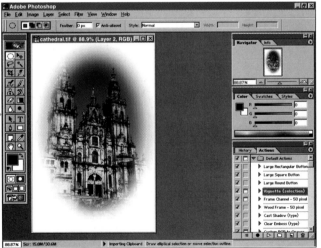

6 Type a pixel value in the Feather Selection dialog box.

Note: The pixel value determines the width of the soft edge of the vignette effect.

7 Click **OK**.

■ Photoshop applies a soft edge around the selection.

CREATE BUTTONS

Photoshop comes with several prebuilt actions that automatically create small buttons on your image.

1 Click **Window** and then **Show Actions** to display the Actions palette.

2 Click the foreground color swatch.

■ The Color Picker dialog box appears.

3 Click to select a foreground color.

Note: This will be the color of the button.

4 Click **OK.**

How can I customize a button that I created with an action?

Because buttons created with Photoshop actions exist in their own layers, you can easily change their size by clicking **Edit**, **Transform**, and then **Scale** (be sure to select the button layer first). You can also overlay a type layer to label a button.

5 Select a button action.

Note: Photoshop comes with prebuilt actions for rectangular, square, and round buttons. In this example, the rectangular action was selected.

6 Click ▷.

■ Photoshop creates a beveled button in the image window.

7 Click the Layers tab in the Layers palette (or click **Window** and then **Show Layers** if the Layers palette is not open).

■ Photoshop creates the button in its own layer, which means that you can easily reposition it in your image.

BATCH PROCESS BY USING ACTIONS

You can apply an action to multiple images automatically with Photoshop's Batch command. The command is a great time-saver for tasks such as optimizing large numbers of digital photos.

BATCH PROCESS BY USING ACTIONS

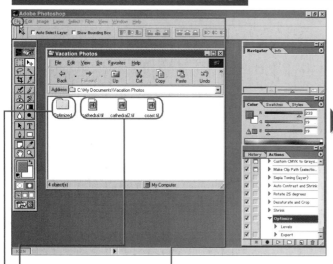

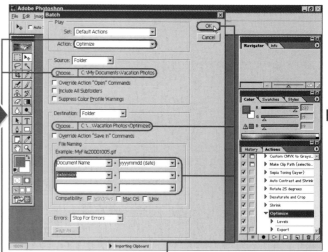

1 Place all the images you would like to apply an action to into a folder.

2 Create a separate folder in which to save your batch-processed files.

■ In this example, an Optimized folder has been created in the same folder as the image files.

3 In Photoshop, click **File**.

4 Click **Automate**.

5 Click **Batch**.

6 Click ▼ and select an action to apply.

■ In this example, an action is being applied that optimizes digital photos.

7 Click **Choose** and select the folder where you have placed your files.

8 Click **Choose** and select the folder where you would like your batch-processed files to be saved.

9 Specify how you would like your batch-processed files to be saved.

10 Click **OK**.

Can I batch process files that I currently have open in Photoshop?

Yes. Just select **Opened Files** from the Source drop-down list in the Batch dialog box. You can have the processed files kept open or saved to a particular folder by selecting the option in the Destination list.

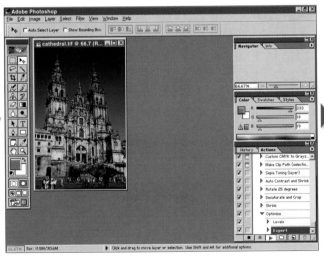

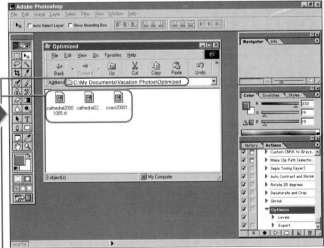

■ Photoshop opens each image in the specified folder one at a time, applies the action, and then saves the files in the destination directory.

■ The processed files are listed in the destination directory.

CREATE A WEB PHOTO GALLERY

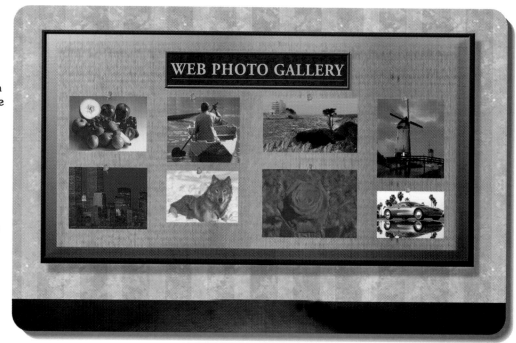

You can have Photoshop automatically create a photo gallery Web site that showcases your images. Photoshop not only sizes and optimizes your image files for the site, but it also creates the Web pages that display the images and links those pages together.

CREATE A WEB PHOTO GALLERY

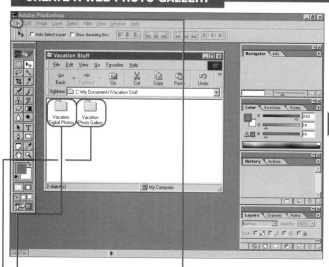

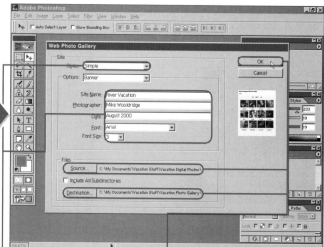

1 Place the images you would like to feature in your photo gallery in a folder.

2 Create a folder where Photoshop can save the image and HTML files.

3 In Photoshop, click **File**.

4 Click **Automate**.

5 Click **Web Photo Gallery**.

6 Click ▼ and select a photo gallery style.

■ Photoshop displays a preview of the style.

7 Enter title information for your Web pages.

8 Click **Source** and select the folder where you placed your original files.

9 Click **Destination** and select the folder where you would like your photo gallery to be saved.

10 Click **OK**.

How can I customize the pages in my Web photo galleries?

You can customize your pages by selecting different gallery styles in the Web Photo Gallery dialog box. The different styles organize the text and images in different ways on the Web pages. Some of the styles organize the gallery content into a framed Web site.

Vertical Frame Style

Table Style

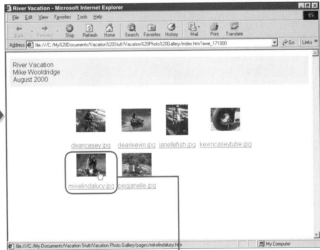

■ Photoshop opens each image in the specified folder, creates versions for the photo gallery, and generates the necessary HTML code.

■ After the processing is complete, Photoshop opens the default Web browser on your computer and displays the home page of the gallery.

11 Click a thumbnail to see a larger version of the image.

CHAPTER 14

Saving Files

Do you want to save your files for use later? Or so that you can use them in another application or on the Web? This chapter shows you how.

SAVE A PHOTOSHOP IMAGE

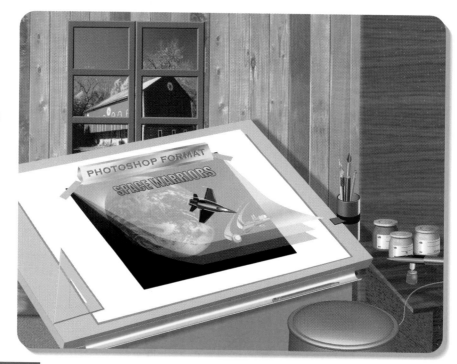

You can save your image in Photoshop's native image format. This format enables you to retain multiple layers in your image, if it has them.

SAVE A PHOTOSHOP IMAGE

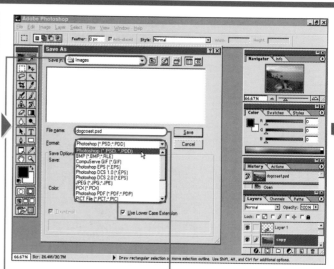

1 Click **File**.

2 Click **Save**.

■ If your file has yet to be named and saved, the Save As dialog box appears.

3 Click ⊡ and choose a folder in which to save the image file.

4 Click ⊡ and select the Photoshop file format.

5 Name the image file.

Note: Photoshop automatically assigns a .psd extension.

How do I choose a file format for my image?

You should choose the format based on how you will want to use the image. If it is a multilayered image and you want to preserve the layers, save it as a Photoshop file. If you want to use it in other applications, save it as a TIFF or EPS file. If you want to use it on the Web, save it as a JPEG or GIF file. For more information on file formats, see the rest of this chapter as well as Photoshop's documentation.

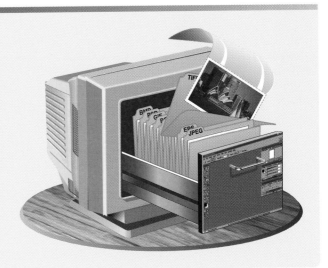

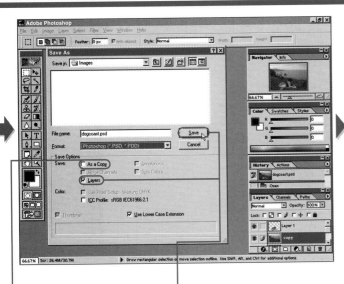

■ If you would like to save a copy of the file and keep the existing file open, click **As a Copy** (☐ changes to ☑).

■ If you would like to merge the multiple layers of your image into one layer, click **Layers** (☑ changes to ☐).

6 Click **Save**.

■ Photoshop saves the image file.

■ The name of the file is displayed in the image's title bar.

SAVE AN IMAGE FOR USE IN ANOTHER APPLICATION

You can save your image in a format that can be opened and used in other imaging or page-layout applications. TIFF (Tagged Image File Format) and EPS (Encapsulated PostScript) are standard printing formats that are supported by many applications on both Windows and Macintosh platforms. BMP (bitmap) is a popular Windows image format, and PICT is a popular Macintosh image format.

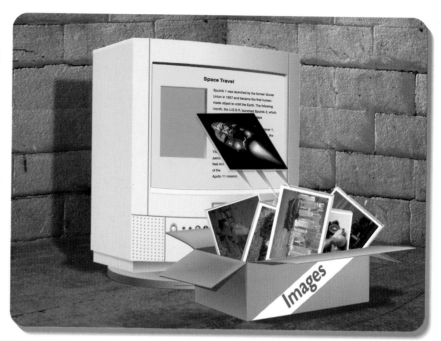

SAVE AN IMAGE FOR USE IN ANOTHER APPLICATION

Note: Most non-Photoshop image formats do not support layers.

1 If your image is in multiple layers, click the Layers ⊙ and click **Flatten Image**.

■ The layers are combined into a single layer.

2 Click **File**.

3 Click **Save As**.

What are some popular page-layout programs that I might use images with?

Adobe PageMaker and QuarkXPress are two popular page-layout programs. They let you combine text and images to create brochures, magazines, and other printed media. You can import TIFF and EPS files saved in Photoshop into both programs.

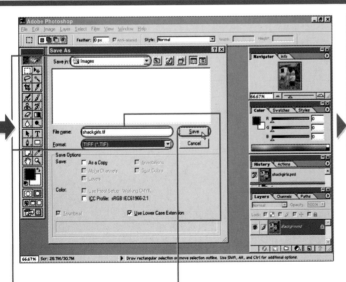

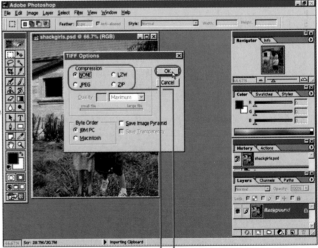

◤ **4** Click ▾ and choose a folder in which to save the image file.

◤ **5** Click ▾ and select a file format.

▶ **6** Type in a filename.

Note: Photoshop automatically assigns an appropriate extension for the file format, such as `.tif` *for TIFF or* `.eps` *for EPS.*

▶ **7** Click **Save**.

■ In this example, the TIFF format was selected. A dialog box appears, enabling you to specify the type of TIFF you would like to save.

■ You can select a compression scheme to decrease the file size of your final TIFF file (○ changes to ◉).

└ **8** Click **OK** to save the file.

SAVE A JPEG FOR THE WEB

You can save a file in the JPEG (Joint Photographic Experts Group) format and publish it on the Web. JPEG is the preferred file format for saving photographic images.

SAVE A JPEG FOR THE WEB

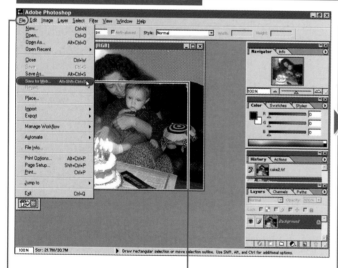

1 Click **File**.

2 Click **Save for Web**.

■ These options let you select a predefined setting or a numeric value from 0 (low quality) to 100 (high quality).

3 Select the JPEG quality settings.

Note: The higher the quality, the greater the resulting file size.

4 Check that the file quality and size are acceptable in the preview window.

5 Click **OK**.

What is image compression?

Image compression involves using mathematical techniques to reduce the amount of information required to describe an image. This results in small file sizes, which is important when transmitting information on the Web. Some compression schemes, such as JPEG, involve some loss in quality due to the compression, but the loss is usually negligible compared to the file size savings.

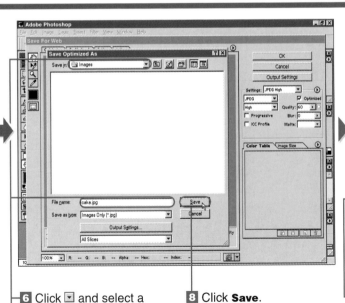

6 Click ▾ and select a folder in which to save the file.

7 Type in a filename.

Note: Photoshop automatically assigns a .jpg extension.

8 Click **Save**.

■ The JPEG file is saved in the specified folder. You can open the folder to access the file.

■ The original image file remains open in Photoshop.

SAVE A GIF FOR THE WEB

You can save a file as a GIF (Graphics Interchange Format) and publish it on the Web. The GIF format is good for saving illustrations that have a lot of solid color.

SAVE A GIF FOR THE WEB

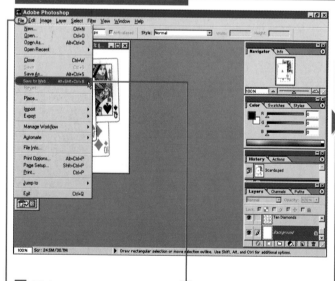

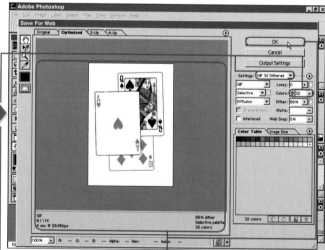

1 Click **File**.

2 Click **Save for Web**.

3 Click ▾ and select a GIF setting.

4 Select the number of colors to include in the image.

5 Check that the file quality and size are acceptable in the preview window.

6 Click **OK**.

Note: GIF allows a maximum of 256 colors, making it unsuitable for many photos.

How do I create GIFs with small file sizes?

The most important factor in creating small GIFs is limiting the number of colors in the final image. (GIF files are limited to 256 colors or fewer.) In images that have just a few solid colors, you can ofter reduce the total number of colors to 16 or 8 without any noticeable reduction in quality.

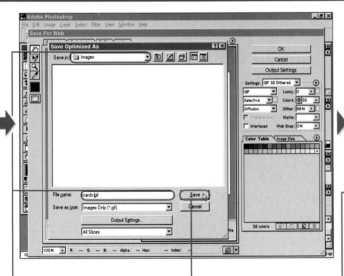

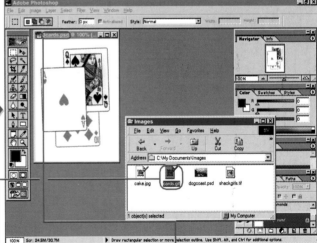

7 Click ▾ and select a folder in which to save the file.

8 Type in a filename.

Note: Photoshop automatically assigns a .gif extension.

9 Click **Save**.

■ The GIF file is saved in the specified folder. You can open the folder to access the file.

■ The original image file remains open in Photoshop.

SAVE A GIF WITH TRANSPARENCY

You can include transparency in files saved in the GIF file format. The transparent pixels do not show up on Web pages.

Because Photoshop Background layers cannot contain transparent pixels, you need to work with non-Background layers to create transparent GIFs. (See Chapter 9 for more about layers.)

SAVE A GIF WITH TRANSPARENCY

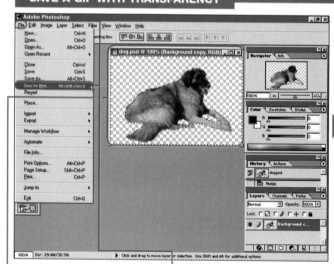

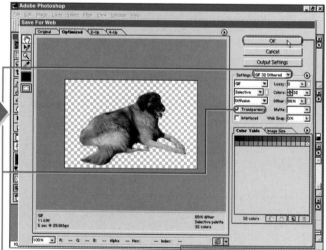

1 Select the area that you want to be transparent with a selection tool.

■ In this example, the dog was selected, and then the selection was inverted.

2 Press Delete to delete the pixels.

■ Photoshop displays a checkerboard pattern where the deleted pixels were. This area will be transparent in the final image.

3 Click **File**.

4 Click **Save for Web**.

5 Click ⊡ and select a GIF setting.

6 Click **Transparency** to retain transparency in the saved file (☐ changes to ☑).

7 Click **OK**.

Can I create transparent JPEG files?

Transparency is not available in files saved as JPEG, the other image format common on the Web besides GIF.

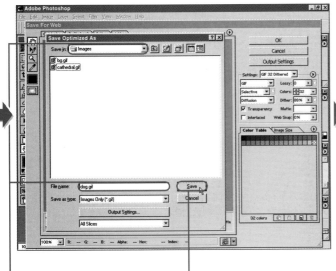

■8 Click ▼ and select a folder in which to save the file.

■9 Name the file.

Note: Photoshop automatically assigns a `.gif` extension.

■10 Click **Save**.

■ In this example, the image has been added to a Web page and opened in a Web browser.

■ The transparency causes the Web page background to show through around the edges of the dog.

SAVE A GIF WITH WEB-SAFE COLORS

You can save your GIF images using only Web-safe colors. This ensures that the images appear the way you expect in browsers running on 256-color monitors.

SAVE A GIF WITH WEB-SAFE COLORS

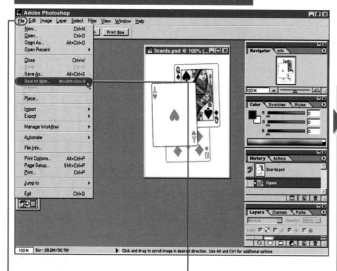

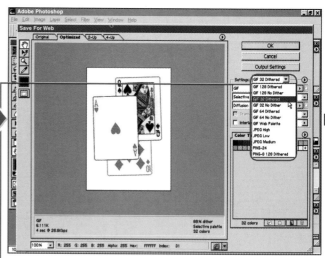

1 Click **File**.

2 Click **Save for Web**.

■ The Save For Web dialog box appears.

3 Click ▾ and select a GIF setting.

Note: You can create Web-safe images only in the GIF format.

Note: When you do not specify Web-safe colors, Photoshop displays the image by choosing from all the colors available in the spectrum.

Should all my Web images be saved with Web-safe colors?

Not necessarily. Nowadays, most people surf the Web on monitors set to thousands of colors or more, which makes Web safety less relevant. Also, it is better to save photographic Web images as non-Web-safe JPEGs because the GIF file format offers poor compression and quality when it comes to photos.

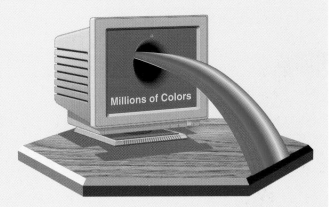

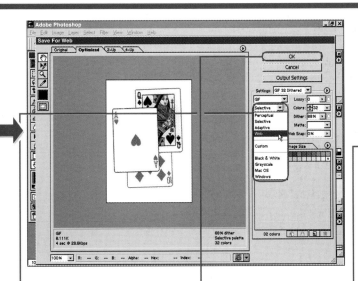

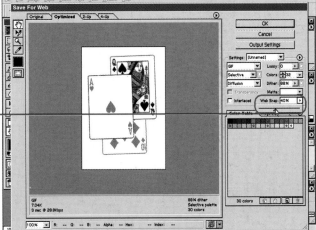

◼ **4** Click ▾ and select **Web** as the color palette type.

◼ Photoshop will now use only colors from the palette available to browsers running on 256-color monitors.

5 Click **OK** to save the image.

MAKE A GIF PARTIALLY WEB-SAFE

◼ You can also specify a degree of Web safety (from 1% to 100%) in your image by using the Web Snap menu.

Note: The Web Snap menu lets you find a compromise between creating a totally Web-safe image (which may display poorly) and an image that has no Web-safe colors at all.

COMPARE FILE SIZES

You can compare the results of different compression schemes on your Web images. This helps you choose which scheme is most efficient and generates the best-looking image. You can then save the image using that scheme.

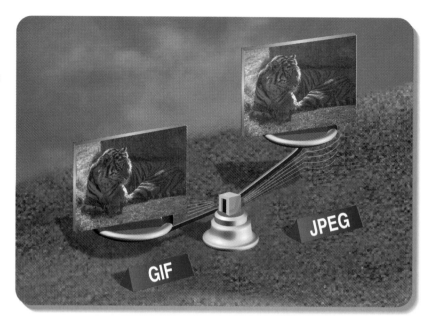

COMPARE FILE SIZES

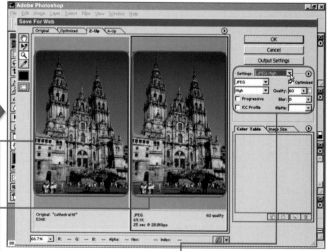

1 Click **File**.

2 Click **Save for Web**.

■ By default, Photoshop displays the optimized version of the image, which is the image with file formatting settings applied.

■ The file size and download time of the optimized version are displayed.

3 Click **2-Up**.

■ Photoshop displays the original image on the left side.

■ Photoshop displays the image with the file formatting settings applied on the right side.

4 To select different settings, click either image and change the settings in the right side of the dialog box.

How do I automatically optimize to a specific file size?

You can click the Settings ⊙ in the Save For Web dialog box and click **Optimize to File Size**. A dialog box appears that lets you specify a final file size for your image. Photoshop then makes the compression adjustments for you to reach that file size.

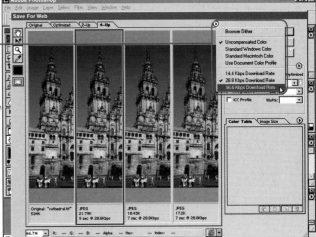

■ Photoshop displays the image with the new settings applied.

■ The new file size is displayed.

5 Click **4-Up** to compare four versions of the image at a time.

■ You can change the modem speed that Photoshop uses to estimate the download time by clicking the top menu ⊙ and selecting different options.

SAVE A SLICED IMAGE

You can save an image that has been partitioned using the Slice tool. Photoshop saves the slices as different images and also saves an HTML file that organizes the slices on a Web page. Slices enable you to save some parts of an image as GIF and others as JPEG. This can result in an overall image that has a smaller file size.

For more information about using the Slice tool, see Chapter 5.

SAVE A SLICED IMAGE

1 Open your sliced image.

2 Click **File**.

3 Click **Save for Web**.

4 Click ▸ (the Slice Select tool).

5 Click one of the image slices.

6 Specify the image settings for the slice.

7 Repeat Steps **5** and **6** for each of the slices.

8 Click **OK**.

How do I publish my Web page online?

After you have created a Web page by saving your sliced Photoshop image, you can make the page available online by transferring the HTML and image files to a Web server. Most people arrange for Web server access through an Internet service provider.

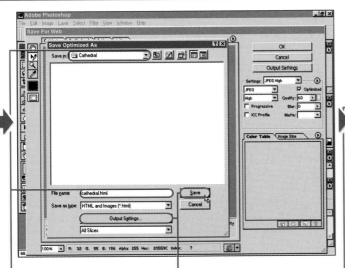

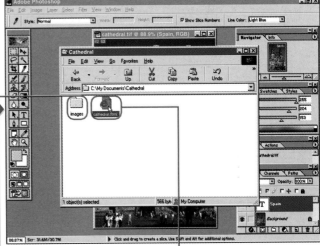

■ **9** Click ⊡ and choose a folder in which to save the files.

■ **10** Name the HTML file that will arrange the slices.

■ Photoshop saves the images by appending slice numbers to the original image name. To change the naming scheme, you can click **Output Settings**.

■ **11** Click **Save** to save the files.

■ You can access the HTML and image files in the folder that was specified.

■ The image files are saved in a separate images folder.

■ **12** To view the Web page, double-click the HTML file.

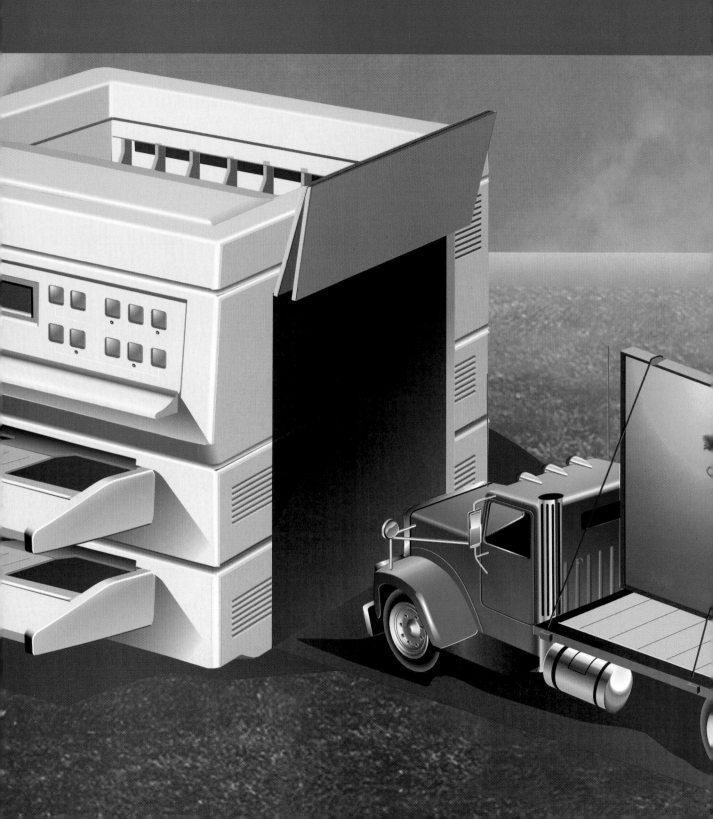

CHAPTER 15

Printing Images

Printing enables you to save the digital imagery you create in Photoshop in hard-copy form. Photoshop can print to black-and-white or color printers.

You can print your Photoshop image in color using color inkjet and dye-sublimation printers.

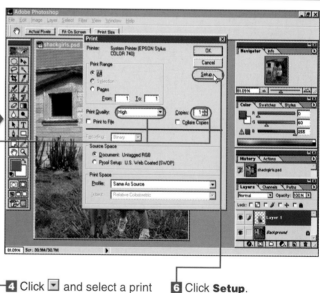

1 Make sure that the layers you would like to print are visible.

Note: An ⬛ means that a layer is visible.

2 Click **File**.

3 Click **Print**.

4 Click ▼ and select a print quality.

5 Click ⬆ to select the number of copies.

6 Click **Setup**.

How do I include my image's filename on my printout?

Click the Caption check box (□ changes to 3) in the Page Setup dialog box to include the filename on your printout.

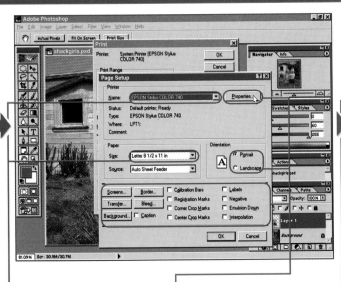

■ The Page Setup dialog box appears.

7 Click ▼ and select a color printer in the Name list.

8 Click ▼ and select a paper size.

9 Select an orientation (○ changes to ⊙).

10 Click **Properties**.

■ The options at the bottom of the dialog box offer advanced prepress printing features.

11 Click **Color** (○ changes to ⊙).

12 Select other properties specific to your brand of color printer.

Note: The Properties dialog box may vary depending on your printer.

13 Click **OK**.

14 Click **OK** in the Page Setup and Print dialog boxes.

■ The image is printed in color.

PRINT IN BLACK AND WHITE

You can print in black
and white on a laser
printer or a color printer
set to black and white.

PRINT IN BLACK AND WHITE

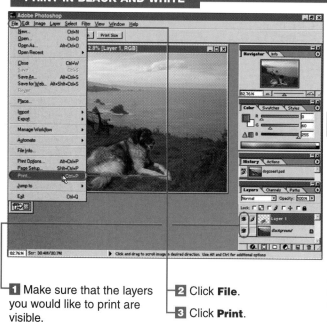

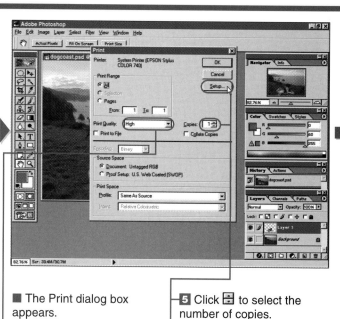

1 Make sure that the layers
you would like to print are
visible.

*Note: An 🔲 means that a layer is
visible.*

2 Click **File**.

3 Click **Print**.

■ The Print dialog box
appears.

4 Click 🔽 and select a print
quality.

5 Click 📶 to select the
number of copies.

6 Click **Setup**.

What is halftoning?

In grayscale printing, halftoning is the process by which a printer creates the appearance of different shades of gray using only black ink. If you look closely at a grayscale image that has been printed on most black-and-white laser printers, you will see that the image is made up of patterns of tiny, differently sized dots. Larger dots produce the darker gray areas of the image while smaller dots produce the lighter gray areas.

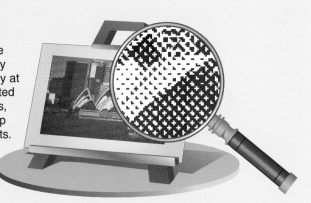

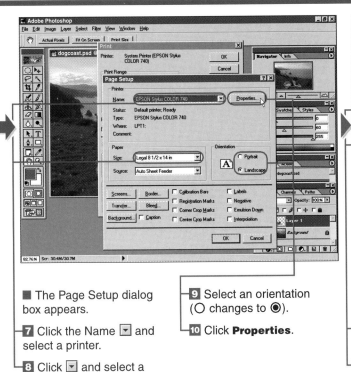

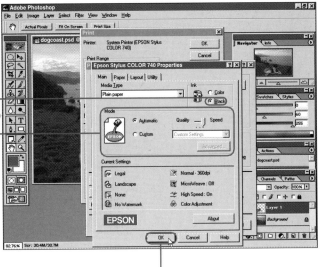

■ The Page Setup dialog box appears.

7 Click the Name ▼ and select a printer.

8 Click ▼ and select a paper size.

9 Select an orientation (○ changes to ◉).

10 Click **Properties**.

■ The Properties dialog box appears.

11 Select black ink or grayscale (○ changes to ◉).

12 Select other properties specific to your brand of printer.

13 Click **OK**.

14 Click **OK** in the Page Setup and Print dialog boxes.

■ The image is printed in black and white.

ADJUST PRINT OPTIONS

Photoshop lets you adjust the size and positioning of your printed image in the Print Options dialog box.

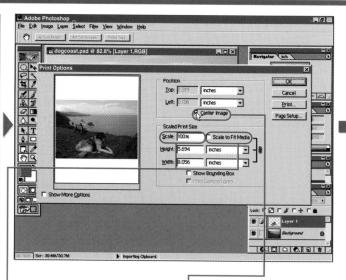

■1 Make sure that the layers you would like to print are visible.

Note: An ⬛ means that a layer is visible.

■2 Click **File**.

■3 Click **Print Options**.

■4 Type a percentage in the Scale box to shrink or expand the image.

■ Clicking **Scale to Fit Media** (☐ changes to ✔) scales the image to the maximum size for the current printing settings.

■5 Click **Center Image** to allow for the repositioning of the image (✔ changes to ☐).

272

How do I set a background color for my printed image?

From the Print Options dialog box, click **Page Setup**. Then click **Background** and use the Color Picker to select a background color. When you print your image, this color fills the space outside the image area on the printed page.

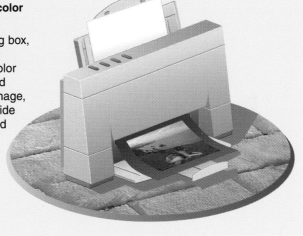

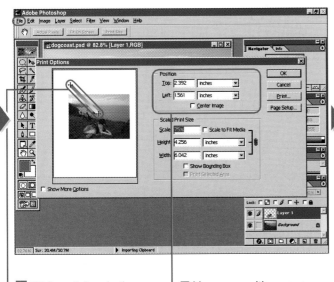

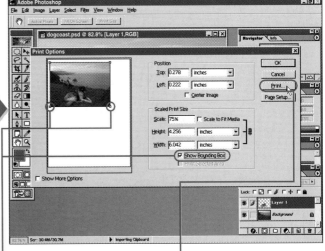

6 Click and drag in the image window to reposition the image on the page.

■ You can position your image precisely by entering values in the Top and Left fields.

7 Click **Show Bounding Box** (☐ changes to ☑).

■ Handles on the image edges enable you to scale the image by clicking and dragging.

8 To print the image, click **Print**.

CREATE AND PRINT A CONTACT SHEET

Photoshop can automatically create a digital version of a photographer's contact sheet that you can print. Contact sheets are made up of miniature versions of images and are useful for keeping a hard-copy record of your digital images.

CREATE AND PRINT A CONTACT SHEET

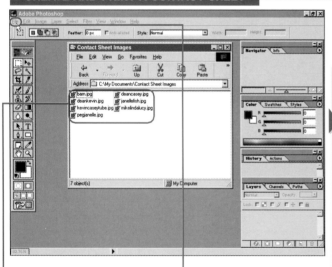

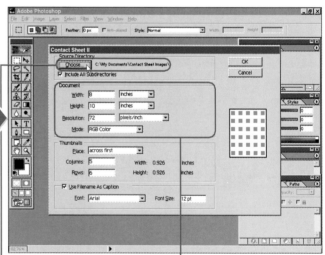

1 Place the images that you would like to put on the contact sheet in a single folder.

2 In Photoshop, click **File**.

3 Click **Automate**.

4 Click **Contact Sheet II**.

5 Click **Choose** and browse to the folder where you have stored your images.

6 Select a size and resolution for your contact sheet. Keep the size within the bounds of the paper that you will be printing on.

How do I create a picture package?

Photoshop can automatically create a one-page layout with a selected image at various sizes — a picture package. Click **File**, **Automate**, and then **Picture Package**. You can choose from more than 30 picture-package layouts.

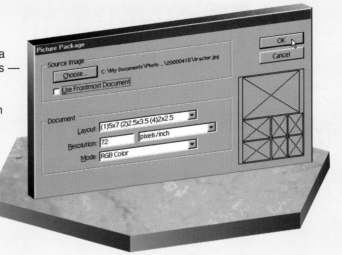

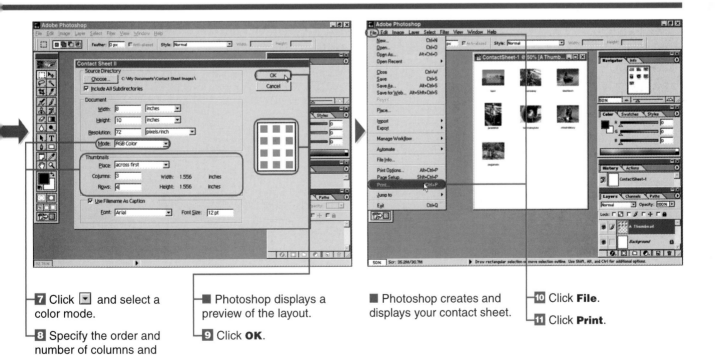

7 Click ▼ and select a color mode.

8 Specify the order and number of columns and rows in the sheet layout.

■ Photoshop displays a preview of the layout.

9 Click **OK**.

■ Photoshop creates and displays your contact sheet.

10 Click **File**.

11 Click **Print**.

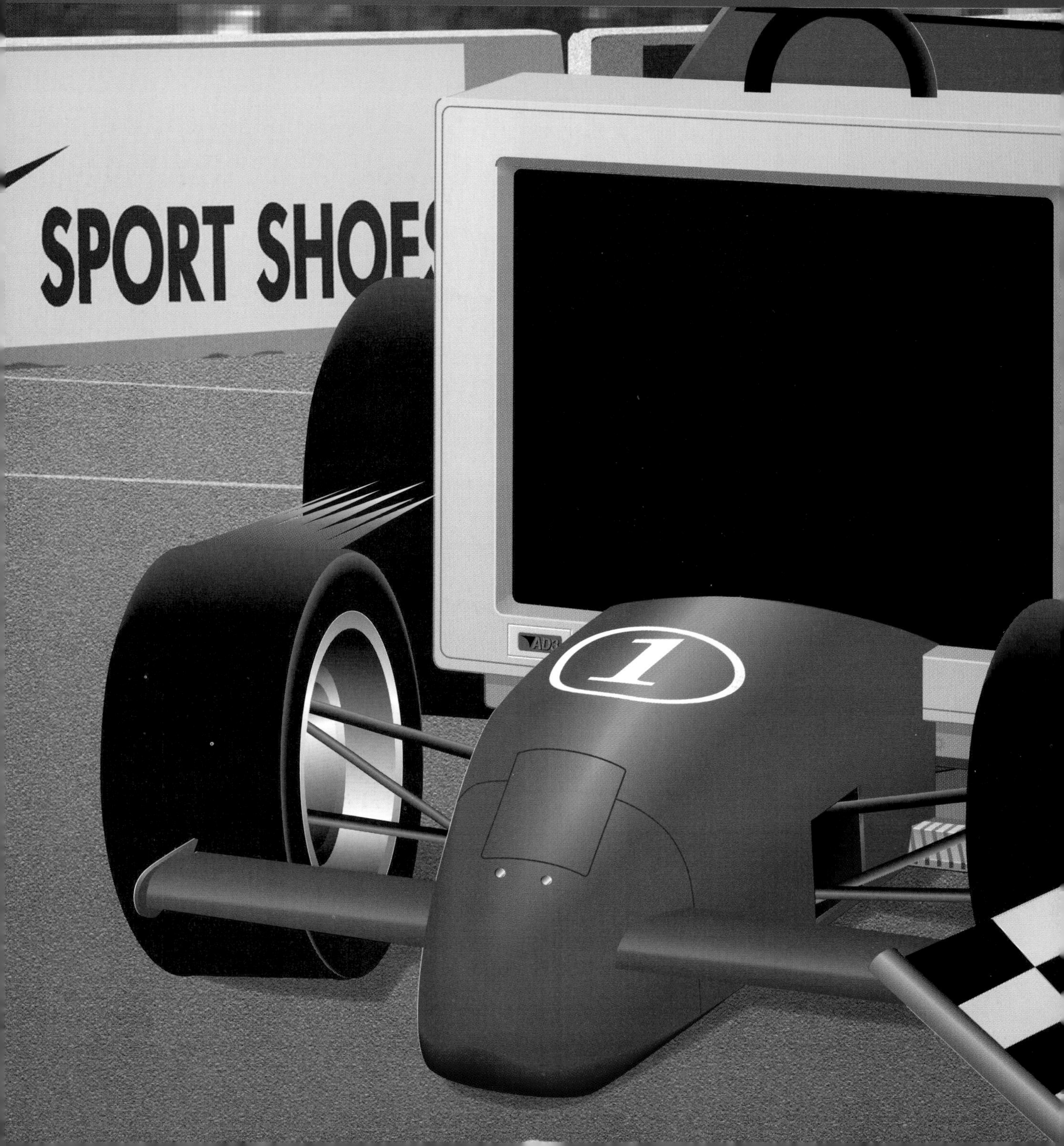
SPORT

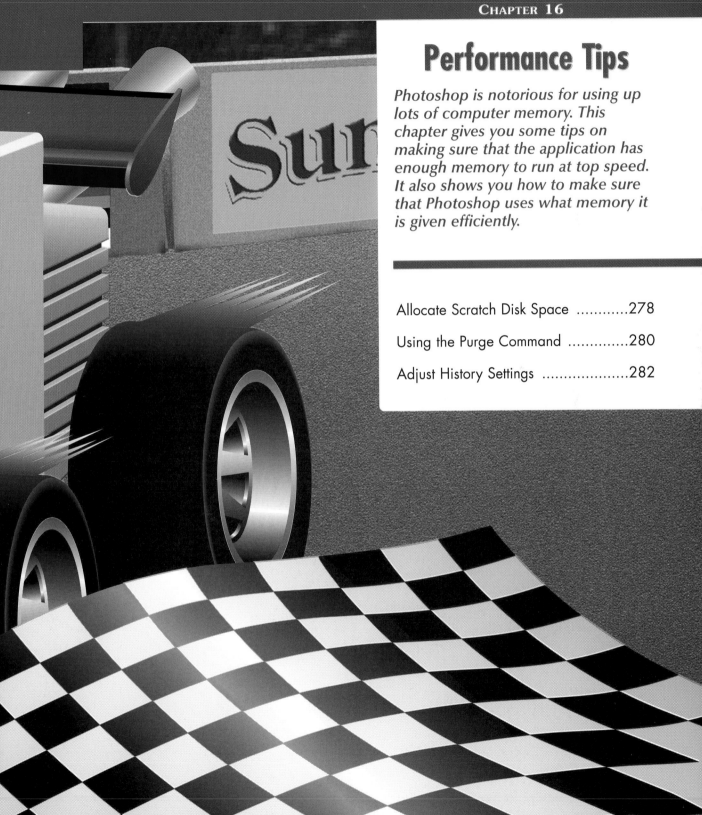

CHAPTER 16

Performance Tips

Photoshop is notorious for using up lots of computer memory. This chapter gives you some tips on making sure that the application has enough memory to run at top speed. It also shows you how to make sure that Photoshop uses what memory it is given efficiently.

ALLOCATE SCRATCH DISK SPACE

You can give Photoshop extra memory (known as *scratch disk space*) from your hard drive to use when it runs out of RAM (random access memory). This can enable you to open up more files at once.

ALLOCATE SCRATCH DISK SPACE

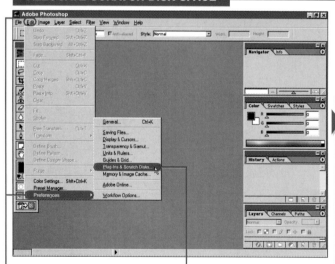

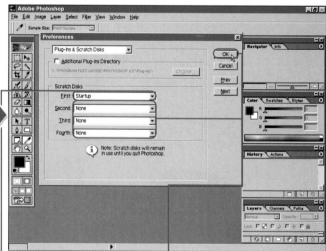

1 Click **Edit**.

2 Click **Preferences**.

3 Click **Plug-Ins & Scratch Disks**.

■ The Preferences dialog box appears.

■ Photoshop uses your startup drive for scratch space by default.

■ If you have more than one hard drive available, you can specify that Photoshop use other drives when it needs to.

Note: You can specify up to four drives, total.

4 Click **OK**.

How do I allocate more RAM to Photoshop?

Click **Edit**, **Preferences**, and then **Memory & Image Cache**. To boost the RAM allocated to Photoshop, increase the Used By Photoshop value. You will need to restart Photoshop for changes to take effect.

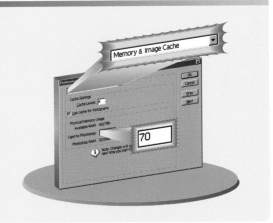

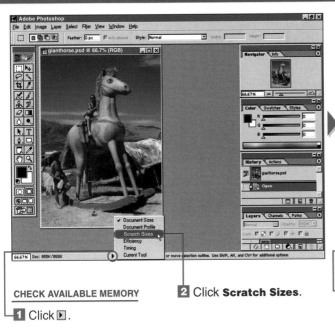

CHECK AVAILABLE MEMORY

1 Click ▶.

2 Click **Scratch Sizes**.

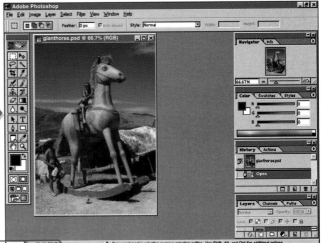

■ The left number is the amount of memory being used by Photoshop. The right number is the total amount of RAM available.

Note: If the left number is greater than the right, Photoshop is using scratch disk space.

USING THE PURGE COMMAND

You can tell Photoshop to free up the RAM it uses to remember past commands so that the memory can be used for other purposes. This can boost Photoshop's speed.

USING THE PURGE COMMAND

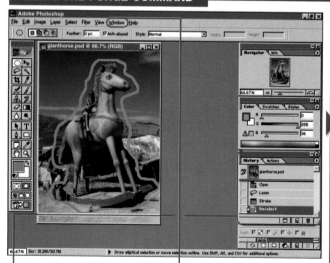

■ Photoshop displays previously executed commands in the History palette. Each command represents information stored in your computer's memory.

■ If the History palette is hidden, you can click **Window** and then **Show History** to display it.

1 Click **Edit**.

2 Click **Purge**.

■ You can purge the previous command (Undo), information stored from a cut or copy command (Clipboard), or the commands stored in the History palette (Histories).

3 To purge all the information, click **All**.

Note: Do not use the Purge command if you still need to use any of the information (to perform a Paste command or undo past commands, for instance).

**Why can freeing up memory
cause Photoshop to run faster?**

When all the available fast
memory (RAM) in your computer
is used up, Photoshop has to start
storing information in your
computer's hard drive memory.
This memory is much slower.
Consequently, purging
Photoshop's memory and keeping
as much RAM free as possible
can keep the application running
at top speed.

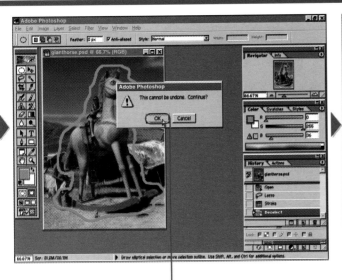

■ Photoshop displays a
warning.

4 Click **OK**.

■ Photoshop purges the
information from its
memory.

■ All the commands but
the most recent one are
deleted from the History
palette.

ADJUST HISTORY SETTINGS

You can control the amount of information stored in the History palette. This enables you to keep that information from taking up too much memory and slowing down Photoshop.

ADJUST HISTORY SETTINGS

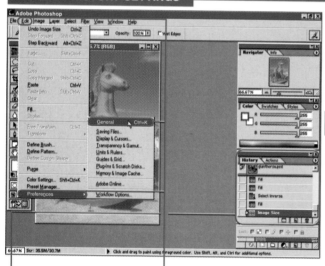

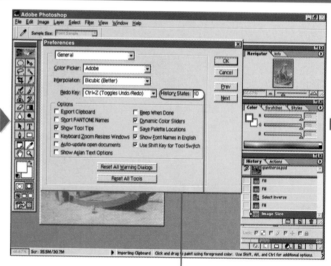

■ Photoshop displays previously executed commands in the History palette.

-1 Click **Edit**.

-2 Click **Preferences**.

-3 Click **General**.

■ The General Preferences dialog box appears.

■ The History States value is the maximum number of commands Photoshop will remember at a time.

Note: To find out how to use the History palette to undo commands, see Chapter 2.

How much RAM (random access memory) does Photoshop need to run efficiently?

When it comes to running Photoshop efficiently, you can never have enough RAM. Multilayered Photoshop files can take up many megabytes of memory when they are opened. Photoshop also uses RAM for every command it stores in its history. Adobe recommends that users have at least 64MB of RAM (as well as 125MB available hard disk space) to run Photoshop, but it is a good idea to have twice that, especially if you are working with large files that have lots of layers.

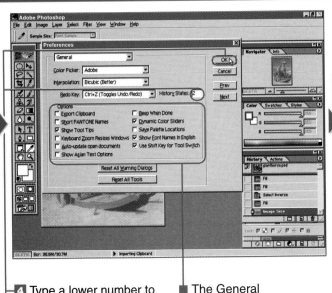

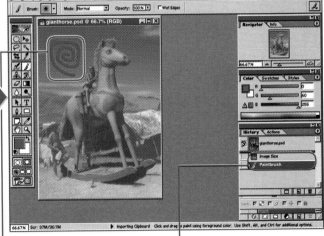

4 Type a lower number to reduce the amount of memory the History palette uses.

5 Click **OK**.

■ The General Preferences dialog box also lets you adjust other useful Photoshop features.

6 Perform a command.

Note: In this example, the paintbrush was used.

■ Photoshop deletes older History commands it had saved.

INDEX

INDEX

INDEX

Read Less, Learn More™

Visual

Simplified®

Simply the Easiest Way to Learn

For visual learners who are brand-new to a topic and want to be shown, not told, how to solve a problem in a friendly, approachable way.

All *Simplified*® books feature friendly Disk characters who demonstrate and explain the purpose of each task.

Title	ISBN	Price
America Online® Simplified®, 2nd Ed.	0-7645-3433-5	$24.99
Computers Simplified®, 4th Ed.	0-7645-6042-5	$24.99
Creating Web Pages with HTML Simplified®, 2nd Ed.	0-7645-6067-0	$24.99
Excel 97 Simplified®	0-7645-6022-0	$24.99
Excel for Windows® 95 Simpified®	1-56884-682-7	$19.99
FrontPage® 2000® Simplified®	0-7645-3450-5	$24.99
Internet and World Wide Web Simplified®, 3rd Ed.	0-7645-3409-2	$24.99
Lotus® 1-2-3® Release 5 for Windows® Simplified®	1-56884-670-3	$19.99
Microsoft® Access 2000 Simplified®	0-7645-6058-1	$24.99
Microsoft® Excel 2000 Simplified®	0-7645-6053-0	$24.99
Microsoft® Office 2000 Simplified®	0-7645-6052-2	$29.99
Microsoft® Word 2000 Simplified®	0-7645-6054-9	$24.99
More Windows® 95 Simplified®	1-56884-689-4	$19.99
More Windows® 98 Simplified®	0-7645-6037-9	$24.99
Office 97 Simplified®	0-7645-6009-3	$29.99
PC Upgrade and Repair Simplified®	0-7645-6049-2	$24.99
Windows® 95 Simplified®	1-56884-662-2	$19.99
Windows® 98 Simplified®	0-7645-6030-1	$24.99
Windows® 2000 Professional Simplified®	0-7645-3422-X	$24.99
Windows® Me Millennium Edition Simplified®	0-7645-3494-7	$24.99
Word 97 Simplified®	0-7645-6011-5	$24.99

Over 9 million *Visual* books in print!

with these full-color Visual™ guides

The Fast and Easy Way to Learn

 Discover how to use what you learn with "Teach Yourself" tips

For visual learners who want to guide themselves through the basics of any technology topic. *Teach Yourself VISUALLY* offers more expanded coverage than our bestselling *Simplified* series.

Title	ISBN	Price
Teach Yourself Access 97 VISUALLY™	0-7645-6026-3	$29.99
Teach Yourself Computers and the Internet VISUALLY™, 2nd Ed.	0-7645-6041-7	$29.99
Teach Yourself FrontPage® 2000 VISUALLY™	0-7645-3451-3	$29.99
Teach Yourself HTML VISUALLY™	0-7645-3423-8	$29.99
Teach Yourself the Internet and World Wide Web VISUALLY™, 2nd Ed.	0-7645-3410-6	$29.99
Teach Yourself VISUALLY™ Investing Online	0-7645-3459-9	$29.99
Teach Yourself Microsoft® Access 2000 VISUALLY™	0-7645-6059-X	$29.99
Teach Yourself Microsoft® Excel 97 VISUALLY™	0-7645-6063-8	$29.99
Teach Yourself Microsoft® Excel 2000 VISUALLY™	0-7645-6056-5	$29.99
Teach Yourself Microsoft® Office 2000 VISUALLY™	0-7645-6051-4	$29.99
Teach Yourself Microsoft® PowerPoint® 97 VISUALLY™	0-7645-6062-X	$29.99
Teach Yourself Microsoft® PowerPoint® 2000 VISUALLY™	0-7645-6060-3	$29.99
Teach Yourself More Windows® 98 VISUALLY™	0-7645-6044-1	$29.99
Teach Yourself Netscape Navigator® 4 VISUALLY™	0-7645-6028-X	$29.99
Teach Yourself Networking VISUALLY™	0-7645-6023-9	$29.99
Teach Yourself Office 97 VISUALLY™	0-7645-6018-2	$29.99
Teach Yourself Red Hat® Linux® VISUALLY™	0-7645-3430-0	$29.99
Teach Yourself Windows® 95 VISUALLY™	0-7645-6001-8	$29.99
Teach Yourself Windows® 98 VISUALLY™	0-7645-6025-5	$29.99
Teach Yourself Windows® 2000 Professional VISUALLY™	0-7645-6040-9	$29.99
Teach Yourself VISUALLY™ Dreamweaver® 3	0-7645-3470-X	$29.99
Teach Yourself VISUALLY™ iMac®	0-7645-3453-X	$29.99
Teach Yourself VISUALLY™ Windows® 2000 Server	0-7645-3428-9	$29.99
Teach Yourself Windows® Me Millennium Edition VISUALLY™	0-7645-3495-5	$29.99
Teach Yourself Windows NT® 4 VISUALLY™	0-7645-6061-1	$29.99
Teach Yourself Word 97 VISUALLY™	0-7645-6032-8	$29.99

The **Visual**™ series is available wherever books are sold, or call **1-800-762-2974.**

Outside the US, call **317-572-3993**

IDG BOOKS ®

TRADE & INDIVIDUAL ORDERS	**EDUCATIONAL ORDERS & DISCOUNTS**	**CORPORATE ORDERS FOR 3-D VISUAL™ SERIES**
Phone: **(800) 762-2974** *or* **(317) 572-3993** *(8 a.m. – 6 p.m., CST, weekdays)* *FAX :* **(800) 550-2747** *or* **(317) 572-4002**	*Phone:* **(800) 434-2086** *(8:30 a.m.–5:00 p.m., CST, weekdays)* *FAX :* **(317) 572-4005**	*Phone:* **(800) 469-6616** *(8 a.m.–5 p.m., EST, weekdays)* *FAX :* **(905) 890-9434**

Qty	ISBN	Title	Price	Total

Shipping & Handling Charges

	Description	First book	Each add'l. book	Total
Domestic	Normal	$4.50	$1.50	$
	Two Day Air	$8.50	$2.50	$
	Overnight	$18.00	$3.00	$
International	Surface	$8.00	$8.00	$
	Airmail	$16.00	$16.00	$
	DHL Air	$17.00	$17.00	$

Subtotal _____

CA residents add applicable sales tax _____

IN, MA and MD residents add 5% sales tax _____

IL residents add 6.25% sales tax _____

RI residents add 7% sales tax _____

TX residents add 8.25% sales tax _____

Shipping _____

Total _____

Ship to:

Name _____

Address _____

Company _____

City/State/Zip _____

Daytime Phone _____

Payment: □ Check to IDG Books (US Funds Only)

□ Visa   □ Mastercard   □ American Express

Card # _____ Exp. _____ Signature _____

*maran***Graphics**™